Shirley Bassey

GREENWICH EDITIONS

Shirley Bassey

MY LIFE ON RECORD AND IN CONCERT

BLOOMSBURY

For Miss Bassey

Personal Manager BEAUDOIN MILLS

Business Manager JOHN WEBBER

Personal Assistant ANDREW McGOWAN

Merchandising by Glenn Orsher WINTERLAND

First published in Great Britain 1998
BLOOMSBURY PUBLISHING Plc, 38 Soho Square, London W1V 5DF

PICTURE SOURCES
Miss Bassey's collection, Tobi Corney, Nicky Johnston/FSP, Philips Records, EMI Records, United Artists Records, London Weekend Television, Hilary Finney, Vivienne, Steen Jacobsen, Kelvin Photos, Las Vegas News Bureau, ABC, Press Association, *New Musical Express*

A CIP catalogue record for this book is available from the British Library

ISBN 0 7475 4090 X

Designed by Bogdan Zarkowski ZARKOWSKI DESIGNS LTD

Printed in Great Britain by Butler and Tanner, Frome and London

Contents

MY LIFE ON RECORD AND IN CONCERT

A few years back I celebrated four wonderful decades in show business, and I'm lucky that, with each passing year, the magic lives on. I hope it does for you too, for my audience is the most precious thing to me. When I walk out on the stage you become the mirror of My Life in Song – a life I would love to share with you in the pages of this book.

Big Spender jets in

BASSEY THE INCENDIARY

Shirley swings in a mauve mini!

OF SHIRLEY BASSEY

Shirley Bassey's Songs Sizzle

WHY SHIRLEY STOLE SHOW

Shirley's Talent Scores

Unbelievable Bassey

BASSEY: GREATEST GIRL IN THE WORLD?

Shirley deserves the ovation

This is my life

Shirley's spectacular

From Star to

Continent to conquer for 'Goldfinger' girl

THE TIGRESS FROM TIGER BAY

A star with her eyes on the stars

Shirley Bassey Remembers Meeting President Kennedy

Shirley Bassey jolts audience

The Bassey Magic

Brilliant Shirley sparkles brighter yet

Demure or sexy, Bassey captivates

SHIR SPECT

Shirl tops big s

The taler Bassey fine voice

Big ticket rush for 'our Shirley's' show

Shirley Bassey Sizzles

1937   8 January. Shirley Veronica Bassey is born.

1937   Brought up in Tiger Bay, Cardiff, Wales, the youngest of seven children.

1942   Starts school in Porthcawl, Wales.

1952   Leaves school and works in the packing department of a sausage factory, supplementing her weekly wage with singing engagements in the local working men's clubs.

1953   Turns professional and makes her début as a professional performer at the Grand Theatre in Luton, Bedfordshire. Joins the touring revue *Memories of Jolson*. Appears for five months in the show *Hot From Harlem*.

1954   Becomes homesick and quits show business to work as a waitress.

1955   Is persuaded to appear at the Astor Club, London, where bandleader Jack Hylton 'discovers' her and books her into the comedian Al Read's West End revue *Such is Life*.

1956   Records her first single, *Burn My Candle,* for the Philips record label.

1957   Makes the British singles charts for the first time with *Banana Boat Song*, reaching number eight. Releases her début album *Born To Sing The Blues*.

1958   *As I Love You* and *Kiss Me, Honey, Honey, Kiss Me* are simultaneously in the Top 10.

1959   Signs to Columbia Records.

1960   *With These Hands* charts on three separate occasions. *As Long As He Needs Me* becomes her first hit single with Columbia Records and stays in the charts for 30 weeks.

1961   *The Fabulous Shirley Bassey* album is released. Becomes established as a cabaret artist in New York and is a success in Las Vegas. Appears at her first Royal Variety Performance.

1962   *Let's Face The Music* album and *What Now My Love* single are released.

1963   Sings for President John F. Kennedy at the White House.

1964   Has a worldwide hit with the James Bond film theme song *Goldfinger*, which sells more than a million copies in the USA alone.

1965   Leaves Columbia and signs with United Artists Records, giving her the freedom to record more in the USA, where she is now established as a major concert and cabaret artist.

1966   Releases *I've Got A Song For You* album.

1967   The immortal *Big Spender* is released as a single.

1968   The release of *This Is My Life*, which has become her personal anthem and normally the closing number at her concerts.

1969   Settles in Switzerland.

Shirley

1970 Sell-out season at London's Talk of the Town nightclub. Releases *Something*, her biggest-selling album so far.

1971 Follow-up album, *Something Else,* repeats the success of *Something*.

1972 *TV Times* names Shirley Bassey "Best Female Singer".

1973 *TV Times* names her "Best Female Singer" for the second year running.

1974 *Music Week* names Shirley Bassey "Best Female Singer".

1976 Celebrates 20 years as a recording artist with a 22-date UK tour. The American Guild of Variety Artists votes her "Best Female Entertainer".

1977 Receives a Britannia Award for "Best Female Solo Singer" for the last 50 years of recorded sound.

1978 Returns to the traditional way of recording – singing live in the studio with full orchestra.

1979 Starts her own BBC TV series which attracts a huge audience.

1981 Announces her semi-retirement, but continues to appear on TV and concert tours.

1982 Releases the album *All By Myself.*

1983 Records *Thought I'd Ring You* with French film star Alain Delon.

1984 Records an album of her major successes, *I Am What I Am*.

1987 Comes out of semi-retirement to collaborate with electro-pop band Yello on *The Rhythm Divine*.

1989 Releases *La Mujer*, an album with all tracks sang in Spanish.

1991 The album *Keep The Music Playing* is released.

1993 Is awarded the CBE by Her Majesty Queen Elizabeth II. The album *Shirley Bassey Sings The Songs Of Andrew Lloyd Webber* is released.

1994 EMI releases *The EMI/UA Years,* a five-CD box set.

1995 Receives the Variety Club of Great Britain's accolade of "Show Business Personality of the Year". Completes her 40th anniversary tour. Releases *Sings The Movies* CD.

1996 Appears on TV in *An Audience with Shirley Bassey*, later released on video. Undertakes her biggest UK tour so far. Has a hit with *Disco* from the Chris Rea film *La Passione*, in which she makes her screen début.

1997 Celebrates her 60th birthday with two open-air concerts which are recorded and released on CD as *The Birthday Concert*.

1998 Appears in the TV Documentary *Shirley Bassey - This Is My Life*. Commences her Diamond Tour.

Bassey

Shirley

15

Born To Sing The Blues

MY BIRTH CERTIFICATE

CERTIFIED COPY OF AN ENTRY OF BIRTH
COPI DILYS O GOFNOD GENEDIGAETH

REGISTRATION DISTRICT }
DOSBARTH COFRESTRU }

1937

BIRTH in the Sub-district o
GENEDIGAETH yn Is-ddosbarth

Columns:— Colofnau:—	1	2	3	4
No.	When and where born	Name if any	Sex	Name and surname of father
Rhif	Pryd a lle y ganwyd	Enw os oes un	Rhyw	Enw a chyfenw'r tad
341	Eighth January 1937 132, Bute Street	Shirley Veronica	Girl	Henry Bassey

CERTIFIED to be a true copy of an entry in the cert
TYSTIOLAETHWYD ei fod yn gopi cywir o gofnod mew
Given at the GENERAL REGISTER OFFICE, LONDON, ur
Fe'i rhoddwyd yn y GENERAL REGISTER OFFICE, LO

the 14 day of April

y dydd o fis

This certificate is issued in pursuance of th
Rhoddir y dystysgrif hon yn unol â Births ar

Section 34 provides that any certified copy o
evidence of the birth or death to which it rel
Office shall be of any force or effect unless
Y mae Adran 34 yn darparu fod unrhyw gop
ei dderbyn fel tystiolaeth o'r enedigaeth ne
ac sy'n proffesu iddo gael ei roddi yn y Swyc

CAUTION:—It is an offence to falsify a
accepted as genuine to the prejudice of any
RHYBUDD:—Y mae'n drosedd ffugio
fwriadu iddi gael ei derbyn fel un ddilys
cyfreithlon.

W/BX 61858

GIVEN AT THE GENERAL REGISTER OFFICE, LONDON.
FE'I RHODDWYD YN Y GENERAL REGISTER OFFICE, LONDON.

Application No. } Y 2934
Rhif y cais }

Cardiff

Cardiff Central   in the County Borough of Cardiff
                    yn

5	6	7	8	9	10*
me, surname and aiden surname of mother / cyfenw a chyfenw norwynol y fam	Occupation of father / Gwaith y tad	Signature, description and residence of informant / Llofnod, disgrifiad a chyfeiriad yr hysbysydd	When registered / Pryd y cofrestrwyd	Signature of registrar / Llofnod y cofrestrydd	Name entered after registration / Enw a gofnodwyd wedi'r cofrestru
iza Jane Bassey ormerly tcalfe	Ship's Fireman (Mercantile Marine)	E.J. Bassey Mother 182, Bute Street Cardiff	Twenty third February 1937	F.W. Lock Registrar	

copy of a Register of Births in the District above-mentioned.

Home

19

THE HOUSE IN TIGER BAY
WHERE I SPENT MY
FORMATIVE YEARS

1948

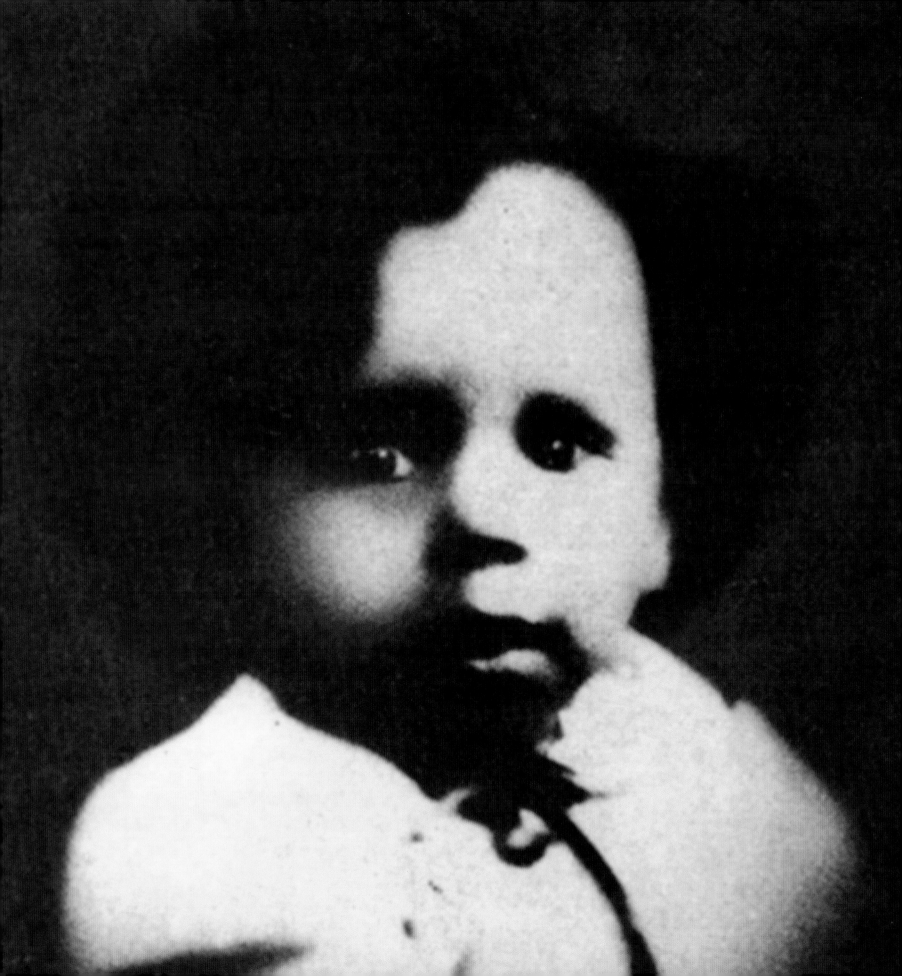

When we were teenagers my brother liked Judy Garland. One day he put on one of her records and that did it for me too. Something went off in my head and my whole body. For me she is the greatest.

When we first met, some years later, I was a great admirer of hers, but I didn't know Judy was of me until she came to see a show of mine in London and asked the waiter to invite me to her table. We bonded right away. I'm going to America for the first time, I told her. Please give me some advice. Should I change my act? Should I have special material written? Because night-clubs in America are different from nightclubs in England. And she said to me, "No, you go with the act that I saw you with tonight. Because you must not do what I did. I listened to everybody and I had lights coming on here and lights going off there and I had costumes and advisers and I ended up like a clown. So you do what I saw you do tonight and you'll be OK."

She was telling me to take a grip on my own career. Which, unfortunately, she couldn't do herself. She had such magic on stage. But not the discipline.

My brother was also a big fan of Billy Eckstine and Sarah Vaughan, and we listened to their records too. He used to do Billy Eckstine and I used to do Sarah Vaughan. I was only about fourteen at the time, but my voice used to come out more Billy Eckstine than Sarah Vaughan. Sarah was another singer with a fantastic technique, but as a jazz singer, Ella Fitzgerald was the best for me. She had warmth and she was so humble. Many years ago I met her after one of her shows at a party they gave for her. I felt so protective towards her because she was so nice and sweet and down to earth and everybody was around her asking for autographs while she was trying to eat. I felt so sorry for her. Please let her enjoy her meal, I told them, and she looked and me and said, 'Thank you very much for that.' I never thought I was going to get the same trouble. I hate it

when people come up to me when I'm eating. To this day it makes me think of what I saw happen with Ella that evening.

As for male singers, Sinatra is way out in front. Incredible. This man holds notes longer than anybody I know, and he once said in a book or an interview that he learnt it from a saxophone player. He saw how sax players breathe. So I gathered that that was his teacher, rather than a vocal coach.

Sinatra used the double-breathing technique. I do it myself sometimes, but I don't know how I do it. It fools my musical director, because he sees me take a breath and thinks, she's going to sing. But I hold the breath and then this note comes out, and to him it's like I'm dou-ble-breathing and sometimes it's a false alarm for him. So he has to watch me, never take his eyes off me, espe-cially when I'm singing out of tempo, because that's when I tend to take a breath, hold it for a while and then sing. I don't know why I do it. But a few musical directors I've had in the past have pointed this out to me. You're doing something very strange, they tend to say. But it works for you, so I'm not going to tell you not to do it, although it is misleading for me as a conductor when I see you breathe. I want to bring in the rest of the orchestra but I've learnt that you're going to take another breath.

Coming back to Sinatra, it's not that he has a specific technique - it's all his own, he made it his own. Nobody taught it to him. He learnt from listening to somebody playing an instrument. I eventually learnt to master what I had by doing vocal exercises with an ex-opera singer, Helena Chanel. Whereas opera singers like Pavarotti, Placido or Carreras, they've been taught. Certainly they all had a voice to begin with, but with opera you have to be taught. All these different operas, different languages and so on. It's a discipline.

Shirley BASSEY

25

The Fabulous Shirley Bassey

In Concert

WILLIAM HENSHALL

VAUDEVILLE AND THEATRICAL AGENT

FIRST CONTRACT

Licensed Annually by the London County Council

TELEPHONE
GERRARD 7667 7668

AFTER 6 P.M.
SPEEDWELL 4278.

TELEGRAMS:
EVELYNCIA,
WESTCENT, LONDON.

101,
CHARING CROSS ROAD,
LONDON, W.C.2.

This Agency is not responsible for any non-fulfilment of Contracts by Proprietors, Managers or Artistes

No. _____

26

An Agreement made the ____ 17th. day of December 19 53

BETWEEN COLUMBIA PRODUCTIONS (hereinafter called "the Management")

of the one part and SHIRLEY BASSEY

(hereinafter called "the Artiste") of the other part. **Witnesseth** that the Management hereby

engages the Artiste and the Artiste agrees to present/appear as known

(or in his usual entertainment) at the Theatre and from the dates for the periods
and at the salaries stated in the Schedule hereto, upon and subject to the terms and
conditions of Schedule I. of the Ordinary form of Contract contained in the Award of
Mr. A. J. Ashton, K.C. dated 22nd September 1919.

1953

SCHEDULE   (Ten Pounds)

The Artiste agrees to appear at   two   performances XXX XXX at a salary of £ 10 : 0: 0

1   Sunday   N.C.O.Club
     Week at   Burtonwood   XXXXXXXXX 20th. December   1953.

Rehearsal at ....

Week at .... commencing .... 19 ......

Rehearsal at ....

Week at .... commencing .... 19 ......

Rehearsal at ....

Week at .... commencing .... 19 ......

Rehearsal at ....

27

MY FIRST CONTRACT,
SIGNED IN 1953,
FOR TWO SHOWS
AT THE NCO CLUB
IN BURTONWOOD,
LANCASHIRE

Bill Matter, etc., to be sent to .... to arrive at

.... not later than twenty-one days before opening

Signature   J. Bussey

Address   437 Seven Sisters Rd.

Printed by THE SEDAN PRESS, Theatrical and General Printers, 138, Vallance Road, E.1.   Bishopsgate 3928 & 4448

PROGRAMME FOR AL READ'S
SUCH IS LIFE LAUGHTER REVIEW,
INTRODUCING ME AS 'BRITAIN'S
NEW SINGING STAR'

ENGLAND'S FINEST THEATRE

NEW THEATRE OXFORD

PROGRAMME

14—STEPPING OUT ... ...
15—BRITAIN'S NEW SINGING STAR   SHIRLEY BASSEY
16—SUCH IS LIFE ... ...   AL READ
17—MINSTREL MELODIES ... ...
(Decor and Costumes by Alec Shanks)

and the John Tiller Girls   JACK TRIPP

WITH THE
ENTIRE COMPANY
—
Dances and ensembles arranged by Joan Davis
Orchestrations by Billy Ternent

Ladies' Costumes executed by Alec Shanks and George Black Ltd.
Workrooms. Miss Shirley Bassey's costumes executed by Lehcar.
Tailoring by Cyril Castle and Angel of Warwick Street. Mr. Al Read's
Tailoring by Stovell & Mason, W.I. Shoes by Anello & Davide and
Vernon Humpage. Scenery built by Brunskill & Loveday Ltd. Painted
Alick Johnstone Ltd. and Edward Delany. Properties by Lovell &
...mmond. Stagecraft and James Tattersall. Draperies by John
...day & Sons Ltd. Special Electrical Equipment by The Strand
...c & Engineering Co. Ltd. Flowers by Floral Decor.

IN THE STAGE SHOW
HOT FROM HARLEM

IN THE TOURING REVUE
MEMORIES OF AL JOLSON

1953/5

PHILIPS

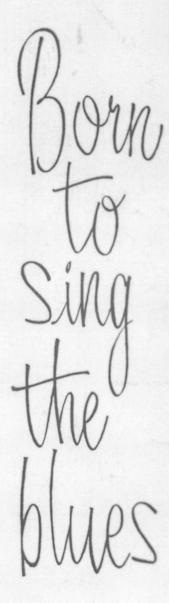

Born to sing the blues

Shirley Bassey

BORN TO SING THE BLUES
BEALE STREET BLUES
WABASH BLUES
BASIN STREET BLUES
BIRTH OF THE BLUES
CARELESS LOVE BLUES
BLUES IN THE NIGHT
THE ST. LOUIS BLUES

The daughter of a West Indian seaman, Shirley Bassey first saw the light of day in Cardiff in 1937. Whilst very young she commenced her stage career as a chorus girl in touring revues but it was soon evident that this young girl possessed great talent.

Before long, she was booked to go on a variety tour as a solo artist and also appear in cabaret. Whilst carrying out a West End engagement in this latter sphere, she had the good fortune to be spotted by Jack Hylton who gave her her biggest break so far by including her in his production *Such Is Life* at the Adelphi Theatre. Her great talent was immediately recognised by the audience and it is no exaggeration to say that she literally 'stopped the show'. The following day the press unanimously declared that a great new star had appeared on the show business horizon.

Some time after this, Shirley had the further good fortune to be spotted by Major Donald Neville-Willing, the impresario, whose responsibility it was at that time to secure the world's greatest stars to appear at the famous Cafe de Paris. He immediately contracted her to appear for him and this, in itself, was a great achievement for any artist so young in years. Once again, Miss Bassey 'stopped the show' nightly and was then hooked for further cabaret in Las Vegas and Hollywood.

After this, a lengthy tour of Australia followed and at all these engagements she proved a sensation.

Shirley Bassey is an extraordinary artist who almost invariably dislikes every new song on sight and says so in no uncertain terms! Possibly this is because she hates learning new songs. Once learnt, however, the situation is entirely different. She readily agrees that she was wrong in the first place about the song concerned and then proceeds to give a performance of it which very few singers in the world today could equal.

Another extraordinary thing about this artist is that no matter whether she has a cold, is tired or even ill, it never appears to affect her singing and even at the end of a long session that lasts for hours, she never shows any signs of tiredness whatsoever.

One of the first numbers she sang on television was a blues number and from this came the idea to present her in an album of all the famous blues songs. We feel sure that the combination of Miss Bassey's consummate artistry and the world famous songs contained herein will make this an album to be enjoyed for many years to come.

John Franz sleeve notes

33

1957

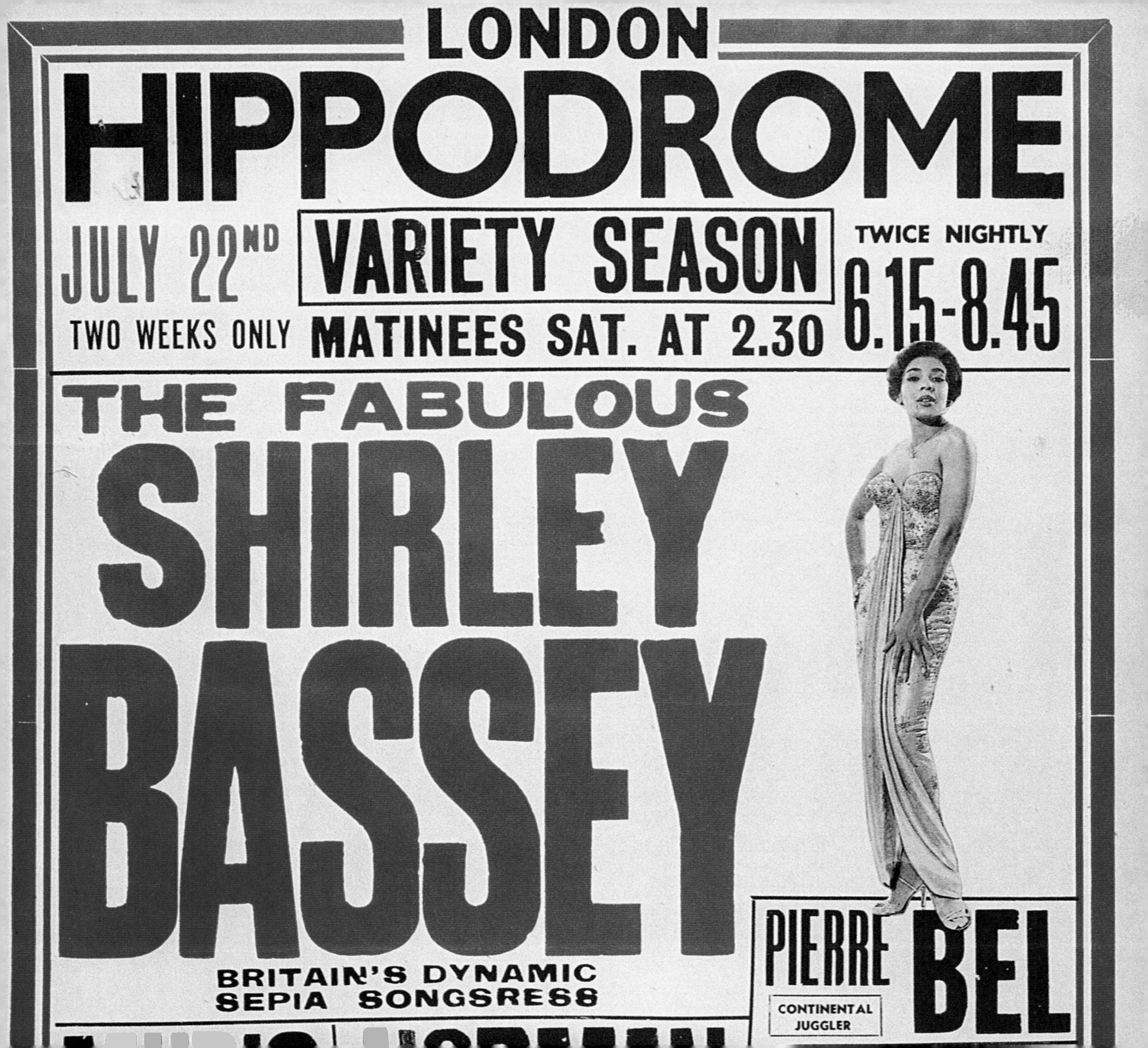
LONDON
HIPPODROME
JULY 22ND
TWO WEEKS ONLY
VARIETY SEASON
MATINEES SAT. AT 2.30
TWICE NIGHTLY
6.15-8.45
THE FABULOUS
SHIRLEY
BASSEY
BRITAIN'S DYNAMIC
SEPIA SONGSRESS
PIERRE BEL
CONTINENTAL JUGGLER

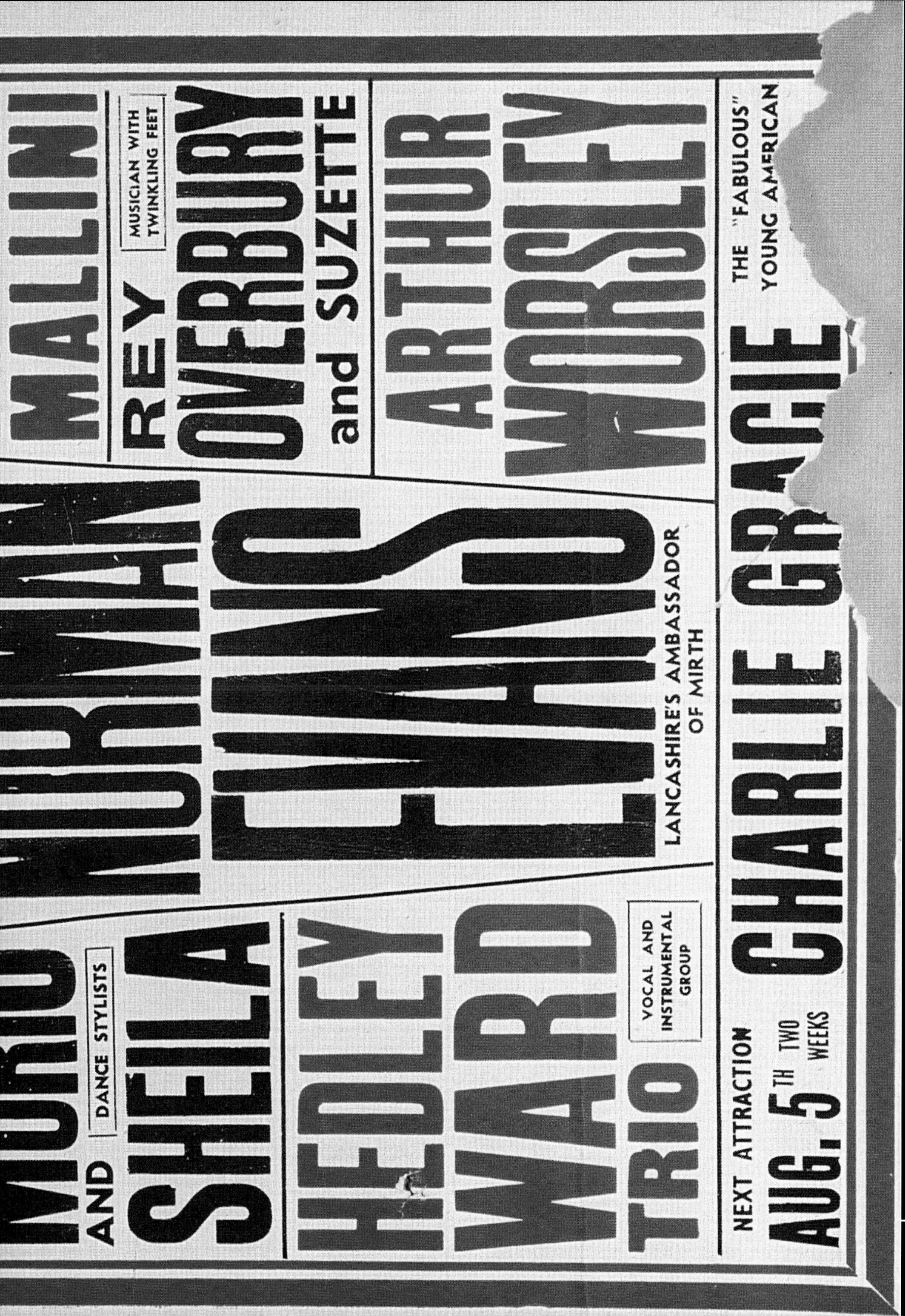

POSTER FOR THE
LONDON HIPPODROME
TWO-WEEK VARIETY SEASON
COMMENCING MONDAY
22 JULY 1957

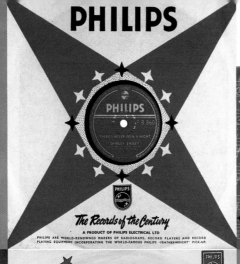
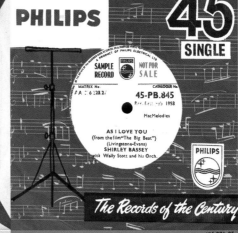

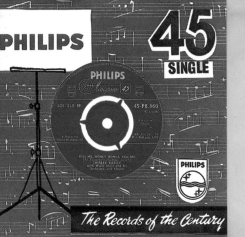

PHILIPS

the bewitching Miss Bassey

PHILIPS

BURN MY CANDLE

NIGHT AND DAY

CRAZY RHYTHM

THE WALL

THE BANANA BOAT SONG

THE GYPSY IN MY SOUL

LOVE FOR SALE

FROM THIS MOMENT ON

KISS ME. HONEY HONEY, KISS ME

YOU, YOU ROMEO

MY FUNNY VALENTINE

HOW ABOUT YOU ?

FIRE DOWN BELOW

AS I LOVE YOU

We just couldn't resist entitling this album *The Bewitching Miss Bassey*, for as all her countless fans throughout the world know, she is indeed bewitching not only on discs but also in the personal appearances in theatres and cabarets which invariably break house records wherever she appears.

It was only 4 years ago that this talented artist made her television debut, and although at that time it was possible to detect traces of inexperience (as is always the case with a newcomer), there was no denying that this girl displayed a tremendous spark which gave promise not only of success in England but also international stardom. This early promise has certainly been fulfilled, for since then she has captivated audiences in New York, Las Vegas, Hollywood, Sydney, Melbourne, Stockholm, Paris, Monte Carlo, etc., and of course in practically every major venue of entertainment in England. The morning after her television debut Philips were fast to sign her to a contract and within the next few weeks she entered a recording studio for the first time in her life to record a song that has been associated with her ever since, namely *Burn My Candle*. Although this record never actually entered the Hit Parade it has over a period of time been a very big seller indeed. This was followed by *The Wayward Wind* which also helped her to gain many more fans; and then came her first really big hit - the famous *Banana Boat Song*. This soared to high places in the Hit Parade and really put Shirley on the map recordwise. Various other records followed, such as *You, You Romeo*, *Fire Down Below* and the very successful EP recording of her act taken during an actual performance at the Cafe de Paris.

During one of her visits to America Shirley recorded in New York under the direction of Mitch Miller, and it is from that session that the song *The Wall* is taken. 1958, however, was destined to be Shirley's biggest year on records for it was during June of that year that she recorded her fabulous version of *As I Love You* which, after a slow start. became No.1 on the Hit Parade, retaining that position for several weeks. In October of 1958 she also recorded the great novelty song *Kiss Me, Honey Honey, Kiss Me* which proved to be another enormous hit and reached the No. 2 spot. These two records were for some time running neck and neck in popularity and she became the first girl singer since 1954 to have two records in the first five of the Hit Parade.

All of these songs (with the exception of *The Wayward Wind*) are contained in this album, together with many other great Bassey performances which display the enormous versatility of this truly international star.

John Franz sleeve notes

1958

EARLY
PUBLICITY
PHOTOS

VARIETY
PROGRAMME
COMMENCING
MONDAY
22 JULY 1957
FOR TWO
WEEKS

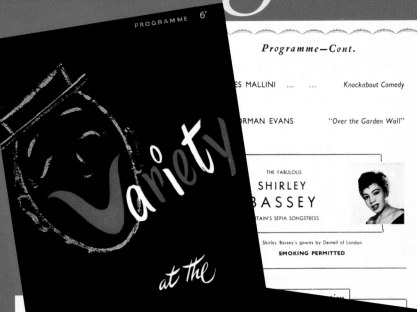

PROGRAMME 6

Variety

at the

LONDON
HIPPODROME

'UKE' SCOTT
Radio and Television's Popular Personality

10

SHIRLEY
BASSEY

BRITAIN'S SEPIA SONGSTRESS

The Management reserves the right to refuse admission to the Theatre and to change, vary
without previous notice, any item of the programme.

In accordance with the requirements of the Licensing Justices...
(a) The Public may leave at the end of the performance by all exits and entrances...
those used as queue waiting-rooms and the doors of such exits and entrances shall
be open. (b) All gangways, passages and staircases shall be kept entirely free from
any other obstructions. (c) Persons shall not be permitted to stand or sit in any
secting gangways. If standing be permitted at the rear of the seating, sufficient s...
left for persons to pass easily to and ro. (d) The fireproof curtain shall a...
maintained in working order and shall be lowered at the beginning of and du...
of every performance.

THIS THEATRE IS DISINFECTED THROUGHOUT WITH JE...

Programme—Cont.

ES MALLINI ... ... Knockabout Comedy

RMAN EVANS "Over the Garden Wall"

THE FABULOUS
SHIRLEY
BASSEY
ITAIN'S SEPIA SONGSTRESS

Shirley Bassey's gowns by Darnell of London
SMOKING PERMITTED

VARIETY

AT THE

HIPPODROME
BIRMINGHAM
- 2 JUN 1958

PROGRAMME PRICE THREEPENCE

2 JUNE 1958
FOUR-PAGE VARIETY PROGRAMME

1957/8

OVERTURE *Michael Collins and his Orchestra and The Williams Singers*

MAKE BELIEVE *Marlys Watters and Don MeKay*

OL' MAN RIVER *Inia Te Wiata*

CAN'T HELP LOVIN' DAT MAN *Shirley Bassey*

LIFE UPON THE WICKED STAGE *Dora Bryan*

YOU ARE LOVE *Marlys Watters and Don McKay*

I MIGHT FALL BACK ON YOU *Dora Bryan and Geoffrey Webb*

WHY DO I LOVE YOU *Marlys Watters and Don McKay*

I STILL SUITS ME *Inia Te Wiata and Isabelle Lucas*

BILL *Shirley Bassey*

FINALE *Dora Bryan, Marlys Watters and Don McKay*

Show Boat is probably one of the most famous musical shows of all time. It seems to have everything that a musical needs—a wonderful story full of romance, excitement, even tragedy, and a score that will surely live forever.

Show Boat was originally based on a bestselling novel by Edna Ferber and the score was magnificently written by Jerome Kern with lyrics by Oscar Hammerstein II. The immortal story of life on a Mississippi Showboat was first presented on Broadway in 1927 and has since been revived many times. As recently as 1951 there was a superb film version by M.G.M.

The score is one of the greatest of all time—included are such wonderful standards as *Ol' Man River, Bill, Only Make Believe* and *Can't Help Lovin' Dat Man*—every one a superb number that gives an artiste the finest opportunity to score a direct hit. When presenting a show such as this on a long playing record the cast is all important and we are particularly fortunate in having the musical talents of so many superb artistes.

Shirley Bassey brings a new magic to *Bill* and *Can't Help Lovin' Dat Man*. Shirley is one of the greatest artistes recording today and this is a new departure for her. It is the first time she has been presented on a Long-Player version of a musical show, but we predict that there will be many future occasions when she will be starring in original cast records of shows specially written for her.

Sleeve notes

1959

Blue Magic

Blue Magic

PRELUDE *(Music by George Posford)*
MALCOLM CLARE, GERALDINE LYNTON
THE DANCERS, THE SHOW GIRLS

BLUE MAGIC .... **SHIRLEY BASSEY**
(Music by Francisco Condé   Words by Ian Grant)

FIRST CAPER .... **TOMMY COOPER**

BIG CITY .... **ARCHIE ROBBINS**
MALCOLM CLARE, GERALDINE LYNTON, THE DANCERS

LEFT BANK MOOD .... **SHIRLEY BASSE**
MALCOLM CLARE, THE DANCERS

(Ballet Music by Reginald Tilsey)

BARCAROLLE *(Music by George Posford   Words by Harold Purc*
MICHAEL GARSON, THE DANCE
and introducing THE THREE K

.... **TOMMY COC**

SEC .... **SHIRLEY BA**
..LCOLM C

T

Blue Magic

A Gay New Glamour Revue

PRINCE OF WALES
PICCADILLY

PROGRAMME
FOR THE
BLUE MAGIC
REVUE

PROGRAMME   SIX DANCE

In Concert

BLUE MAGIC, LONDON

45

1959

SHIRLEY BASSEY'S GREATEST HITS

COLUMBIA

BASSEY Spectacular

TWO
FOR THE PRICE OF
ONE

SHIRLEY BASSEY
with Wally Stott
and his Orchestra and Chorus

PHIL
mono

SHIRLEY BASSE

Sings The Hit Song From
OLIVER!
"AS LONG AS
HE NEEDS ME"
PLUS
Other Popular Selections

ORCHESTRA CONDUCTED BY
NELSON RIDDLE
COURTESY CAPITOL RECORDS

SHIRLEY BASSEY SINGS HITS FROM OLIVER · UNITED ARTISTS UAL 3237 MONAURAL

SHIRLEY BASSEY

BORN TO SING THE BLUES STORMY WEATHER THE WAYWARD WIND
ZUH LEEZI · MISTER BROWN, MISTER JONES, MISTER SMITH
BIRTH OF THE BLUES · BURN MY CANDLE
THE BANANA BOAT SONG

LOVE FOR SALE KISS ME, HONEY, HONEY, KISS ME
YOU, YOU ROMEO FIRE DOWN BELOW
AS I LOVE YOU

GOLDFINGER—Original Motion Picture Score

mono

IAN FLEMING'S
GOLDFINGER

SEAN CONNERY
as JAMES BOND

HONOR BLACKMAN
as PUSSY GALORE
GERT FROBE
as GOLDFINGER

Title Song sung by
SHIRLEY BASSEY

Lyrics by
LESLIE BRICUSSE
& ANTHONY NEWLEY

Music composed, arranged and
conducted by
JOHN BARRY

columbia EMI

shirley
On R
ALBUMS   I 9

stops
th
show

Fontana
special

FROM THIS MOMENT ON
SHIRLEY
BASSEY

SHIRLEY BASSEY

I'VE GOT A SONG FOR YOU

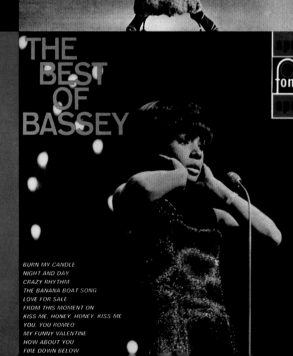
special

THE
BEST
OF
BASSEY

fonta
special

BURN MY CANDLE
NIGHT AND DAY
CRAZY RHYTHM
THE BANANA BOAT SONG
LOVE FOR SALE
FROM THIS MOMENT ON
KISS ME, HONEY, HONEY, KISS ME
YOU, YOU ROMEO
MY FUNNY VALENTINE
HOW ABOUT YOU
FIRE DOWN BELOW

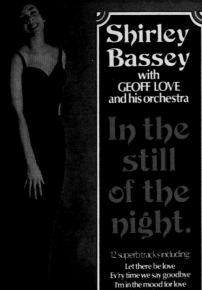

Shirley Bassey
with GEOFF LOVE
and his orchestra

In the still of the night.

12 superb tracks including:

Let there be love
Ev'ry time we say goodbye
I'm in the mood for love
So in love

UNITED ARTISTS

INCLUDES THE HIT
GOLDFINGER

SHIRLEY BASSEY BELTS THE BEST !

GOLDFINGER (GOLDFINGER) **SOMETHING WONDERFUL** (THE KING AND I)
HE LOVES ME (SHE LOVES ME) **IF EVER I WOULD LEAVE YOU** (CAMELOT)
EVERYTHING'S COMING UP ROSES (GYPSY) **A LOT OF LIVIN' TO DO**
(BYE BYE BIRDIE) **PEOPLE** (FUNNY GIRL) **THE SWEETEST SOUNDS** (NO STRINGS)
ONCE IN A LIFETIME (STOP THE WORLD - I WANT TO GET OFF) **SOMEWHERE**
(WEST SIDE STORY) **I COULD HAVE DANCED ALL NIGHT** (MY FAIR LADY)
I BELIEVE IN YOU (HOW TO SUCCEED IN BUSINESS WITHOUT REALLY TRYING)

fontana
special

Born To Sing The Blues
SHIRLEY BASSEY

Born To Sing The Blues
Tonight My Heart She Is Crying
Hands Across The Sea
There's Never Been A Night
Basin Street Blues
Stormy Weather
The Gypsy In My Soul
Blues In The Night
The Wayward Wind
Basin Street Blues
Puh-leeze Mister Brown
Birth Of The Blues

SHIRLEY BASSEY
As long as he needs me

ecord

0s & 1960s

The Original Sound Track Album of
THE LIQUIDATOR
Music composed and conducted by
LALO SCHIFRIN

MCA Classic SOUNDTRACKS

featuring
SHIRLEY BASSEY
Singing the Title Theme

C 048-50 634

SHIRLEY BASSEY
ALL OF ME

Tonight
Moon River
A Foggy Day
Love Is A Many
Splendored Thing
I'm In The Mood For Love
etc.

emidisc

THE SINGLES ALBUM
SHIRLEY BASSEY

shirley bassey
BIG SPENDER

including THE IMPOSSIBLE DREAM, THATS LIFE, IT MUST BE HIM,
IF YOU GO AWAY, ON A CLEAR DAY YOU CAN SEE FOREVER

Shirley Bassey
Songs of Love

I just want to carry on singing and finding unusual songs, songs that challenge. Wearing those glamorous gowns, making people happy, seeing people stand up - which is the greatest thing in the world. It's better than sex, because it lasts so long after I've come off stage, and it can even last until the next day. It gets me on such a high. It's what every singer, every entertainer, dreams about. A standing ovation. It's a tremendous feeling, because it means you've pulled it off, you've done the job so well that these people are standing and telling you so.

You have to learn to deal with the anticlimax too, especially at the end of a tour. It takes me three or four days to get over it. I go home to my apartment and if I wake up in the middle of the night and I want to go to the kitchen, I find myself in my closet. I'm totally disorientated. Come six o'clock in the evening, I'm normally getting ready for the show. When the sun is going down, that's the time I start to get agitated, because I know I'm going on stage. But when the shows are over and I go home, at six o' clock part of my brain says, hey, wait a minute, you're not doing a show tonight. That's the most dreadful moment. It's like you hit rock bottom. Performing is like a drug.

I still get those feelings today, but not in a bad way. I'm not down, and I don't get moody. That's what a drug addict would feel like. I don't mean that. You have a natural down. But it's a confusing down, disorientating. In the end you just have to say to yourself, "Oh gosh, I'm not going on tonight."

I love what I do because I get a feedback. I've worked alone, which is terribly rewarding, and I've been in shows where I've been surrounded by other performers, and that's real teamwork. But since I've been on my own I've learned a tremendous amount about music. And about presentation. I don't even know that I'm doing it, but friends come backstage and say, did you realize that you did so and so? You held in your breath, they say. And they tell me about my body movements, but sometimes I'm not even aware of those movements, because I'm so carried away. Not every night, though. That depends on the audience.

What's so important is the ability to touch them in such a way that they respond to you. Not only the men, but the women too. I find it absolutely terrific. And the children who're there, that's something I'm constantly amazed at.

I love to go right into the audience: touch people, shake hands with them, take their gifts, their flowers. They like that. There are security men who ask me not to do it, because there was one women who, when I shook hands with her, was so strong that she nearly pulled me right into the audience. But I still like to do it.

49

Shirley

B A S E Y

51

This Is My Life

A FOGGY DAY IN LONDON TOWN
I'VE GOT YOU UNDER MY SKIN
CRY ME A RIVER
APRIL IN PARIS
I'VE NEVER BEEN IN LOVE BEFORE
THE MAN THAT GOT AWAY
'S WONDERFUL
I'LL REMEMBER APRIL
EASY TO LOVE
NO ONE EVER TELLS YOU
THEY CAN'T TAKE THAT AWAY FROM ME
THE PARTY'S OVER

The word "fabulous" is probably the most over-worked and mix-used adjective in present-day show business. Many are called "fabulous" but few can really live up to the reputation. We do not hesitate to describe SHIRLEY BASSEY in this way when presenting this wonderful record.

Shirley Bassey's visits to the recording studios created an electric atmosphere of anticipation that prevailed among all the personnel connected with the session—the musicians, the recording engineers and the studio staff. The control room of the studio never had so many visitors calling in with the slightest excuse just to see and hear this great artiste.

Shirley's rise to fame is already one of the outstanding stories of the present day. She was born in Cardiff in 1937 and before she was 21 years of age had achieved a world-wide reputation, appearing in Las Vegas, Hollywood, New York, Stockholm, Monte Carlo, Sydney and Melbourne. In England she is one of the greatest artistes to have appeared during recent years.

Her first great impact was made when famous impresario, Jack Hylton, included her in his Adelphi Theatre, London, production *Such Is Life*. She was an overnight sensation, literally "stopping the show" and winning national press acclaim from all theatre critics the next morning.

From then on Shirley went from strength to strength—triumphant in all fields of entertainment—theatre, revue, television, cabaret and records.

Although this is her first recording for Columbia, she recently held the number one and three spots in the hit parade with her now famous recordings of *As I Love You* and *Kiss Me, Honey, Honey, Kiss Me*.

Listeners to this LP will immediately appraise the great variety of style and interpretation with which Shirley approaches her songs, from the swinging *A Foggy Day In London Town* to her very moving and sentimental approach to *The Party's Over*.

Shirley is also the first to praise the excellent arrangements of musical director, Geoff Love. Geoff has been responsible for the accompaniments of many artistes—too numerous to mention them all—but he can praise none more highly than Shirley Bassey. Immediately this record was completed Geoff said " When do we begin another?"

We feel sure you will say the same when you listen to THE FABULOUS SHIRLEY BASSEY.

Sleeve notes

1961

mono

The fabulous

SHIRLEY BASSEY

COLUMBIA
LONG PLAYING 33⅓ R.P.M. RECORD

★ BON VOYAGE TO BRITAIN'S No.

Shirley Bassey reaches

BRITAIN has produced few musical stars of truly international status during the past quarter of a century, but there's no doubt that Shirley Bassey is among the elite band of world-beaters. And now she's off to America to help cement that claim. In just under a fortnight's time she makes her New York cabaret debut—at the exclusive Persian Room of the lush Plaza Hotel.

While we are all hoping that she will take New York by storm, I'm sure we needn't worry. I'm absolutely convinced that she will prove a resounding success, and add greatly to British musical prestige in the States.

Right now, Shirley has no other American plans apart from this five-week cabaret stint. But it could well be that she will be sought for radio and television appearances, especially as her first release on the United-Artists' label over there coincides with her visit.

"I should dearly love to do some more television in the States," Shirley told me when we chatted in her dressing room at Manchester's Free Trade Hall on Sunday. This was her last appearance before setting off on Wednesday for her U.S. mission.

"But," she went on, "I have my doubts as to whether it could be fitted in during this visit. You see, they book so far ahead over there. For instance, my cabaret season was actually arranged last Christmas, when I was in America for the Ed Sullivan Show."

She can't, in fact, stay long in New York when her Persian Room engagement ends because she has to be back in London to headline ATV's "Sunday Night At The London Palladium" early in November.

"I'd love to appear on the Perry Como Show," Shirley confessed. And maybe that is not such a pipe dream, after all.

Shirley says it with flowers

WHEN she completed her Blackpool season the previous night, Shirley had left in her dressing room an enormous basket of flowers for Alma Cogan, who was playing a Sunday concert there the following day.

"I had a few left over, which I thought you might like," wrote Shirley on the accompanying card, in that tongue-in-cheek manner which she and Alma always adopt when they are having a chuckle at each other's expense.

And as I sat with Shirley in Manchester, a special messenger delivered a note from Alma in Blackpool. "Thanks for the flowers," it read. "They're a little heavy, but I'm wearing them on my dress tonight!"

Ambition

But I discovered that Shirley has one ambition, even stronger than this. **She wants to make a film.**

What's more, she is anxious that the film in question should give her ample opportunity as a dramatic actress.

"I suppose it's the ambition of all singers to prove their worth as actors," she mused. "Certainly, it's mine! I wouldn't mind if the film were a musical or straight—just so long as it gave me a chance to act."

At this point Shirley's husband, Kenneth Hume, joined in. " honestly believe the general publi will be very pleasantly surprised b Shirley's acting ability," he sai " And I'm pretty sure they will b able to judge for themselves withi a year!"

GIRL SINGER, OFF TO AMERICA ★
for Broadway stardom

NMExclusive

interview by
DEREK JOHNSON

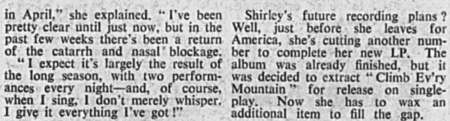

in April," she explained. "I've been pretty clear until just now, but in the past few weeks there's been a return of the catarrh and nasal blockage.

"I expect it's largely the result of the long season, with two performances every night—and, of course, when I sing, I don't merely whisper. I give it everything I've got!"

Thirty minutes later, Shirley was again giving it everything she'd got, to nearly 3,000 highly appreciative Mancunians. I have to admit that I've seldom heard such a tumultuous welcome.

And she responded magnificently—going through every single arrangement she had with her.

Then, with the audience still screaming for more, and having utilised all her music, she launched into an unaccompanied "My Funny Valentine," which really brought the house down.

Shirley's performance and her current smash hit, "Reach For The Stars," was particularly significant. Believe it or not, this was the first time she had sung it to a live audience.

Surprise

Indeed, it was the first time she had sung it at all, since the evening when she recorded it for Columbia.

"I've done absolutely no work on the song," Shirley said. "So that makes it all the more thrilling—as well as a little surprising—that it's doing so well in the charts.

"I've been singing 'Climb Ev'ry Mountain' for some weeks now. I was amazed when it first jumped into the hit parade, as we were so late recording it—but subsequently I've been putting in a lot of work on it, and now invariably it's the hit of my act."

Shirley's future recording plans? Well, just before she leaves for America, she's cutting another number to complete her new LP. The album was already finished, but it was decided to extract "Climb Ev'ry Mountain" for release on single-play. Now she has to wax an additional item to fill the gap.

I find the fact singularly refreshing. There are very few artists and recording managers who seem to worry about the duplication of songs on singles and LPs. Shirley has no plans for cutting any further singles before she departs for America.

Disc plans

"It will probably be my first job when I get back in the autumn," she said. "But I don't want to hurry things along too quickly. I'm very happy with two songs in the sellers at the moment, and I don't intend to force myself on the public. I propose to let it rest for a few weeks."

I remarked to Shirley that, unlike many male singers who seem to lose fans when they marry, her following had certainly not diminished.

"I've thought a lot about that," she replied. "And I can only suppose it's because most of the record-buyers are girls. The majority of my fan letters certainly are from girls."

So Shirley leaves for the hard-boiled entertainment centre of New York. "If my audience there are one quarter as good as you, I shall be well satisfied," she told the Manchester crowd on Sunday.

Well, I'm sure they will be. And I'm equally certain that all NME readers will want to wish Shirley bon voyage, and lots of luck.

You know, I was all set to make film about six months ago," Shirley ed. "Then I had my tonsil able, and was out of action for while, so the project was temporarily shelved."

asked Shirley how her throat I was well aware that last week had a couple of days off from summer season show in Black-

Those two nights were the first I'd had off since my operation

mono

COLUMBIA
LONG PLAYING 33⅓ R.P.M. RECORD

Shirley

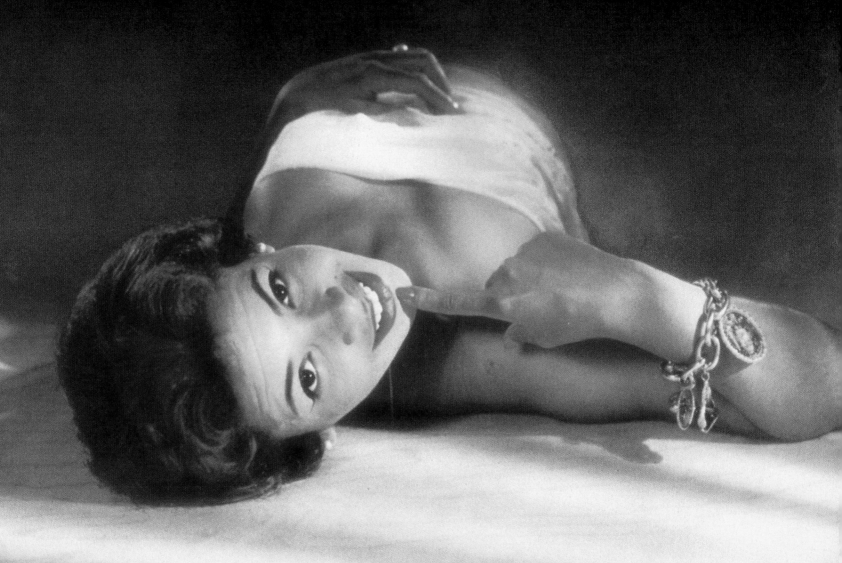

IN THE STILL OF THE NIGHT
LET THERE BE LOVE
ALL AT ONCE (DEJA)
FOR EVERY MAN THERE'S A WOMAN
I'M IN THE MOOD FOR LOVE
SO IN LOVE
IF I WERE A BELL
THERE WILL NEVER BE ANOTHER YOU
HOORAY FOR LOVE
TOO LATE NOW
I'M SHOOTING HIGH
EV'RY TIME WE SAY GOODBYE

Shirley Bassey has now reached the stage of her career where she is firmly established as an assured international star. There are few performers who are immediately recognisable by their christian name, but mention Shirley to any member of the public and they know at once that one is referring to the fabulous Shirley Bassey.

In no time at all this exciting personality from Tiger Bay, Cardiff, has risen to the heights of great vocalists. She has created many hit songs and appeared in the greatest entertainment centres of the world. At the close of 1960 she was a great success in New York, and is scheduled soon to appear in her first musical comedy. All this is a far cry from the young 16-year-old who was discovered singing in a club in Cardiff, and then booked to appear in a show called *Hot From Harlem*, after which Shirley returned to Cardiff and got a job as a waitress.

Shirley originally disliked Show Business because it kept her away from her family and she got homesick. It was her mother who persuaded her to return to the world of entertainment and Shirley eventually arrived in London to start rehearsals for a new show. After working about six months in variety as a solo act she appeared at the Astor Club in London, where she was seen by Jack Hylton and booked for his revue *Such Is Life* at the Adelphi Theatre.

After the Adelphi she played the Cafe de Paris, El Rancho in Las Vegas, Ciro's in Hollywood and the Marino Riverside Hotel. She has also toured Sweden, Holland, Belgium, played at the Sporting Club in Monte Carlo and eventually in Sydney and Melbourne, Australia.

Shortly after her return to England she starred at the Prince of Wales Theatre in *Blue Magic*, during which time she was constantly at the top of the Hit Parade with *Banana Boat Song*; *Kiss Me Honey, Honey, Kiss Me*: *As I Love You* and *Love For Sale*. Since she joined Columbia Records she has scored with *With These Hands*, *The Party's Over* and, recently, smashed to the top with *As Long As He Needs Me*, the hit song from Lionel Bart's fabulous musical *Oliver*.

This is Shirley's second LP for Columbia. Her first, *The Fabulous Shirley Bassey*, has been issued all over the world including Canada and America where she is exclusively signed to M.G.M.

Supporting Shirley's incredible vocal performances is the wonderful orchestra of Geoff Love. Geoff's brilliant arrangements have long been a hallmark of quality and success in the recording world and he is never happier than when he is working with "Shirley".

Sleeve notes

1961

THEATRE PROGRAMME
FOR A TWO-WEEK
SEASON OF VARIETY
WITH SUPPORT ACTS
INCLUDING
MIKE & BERNIE WINTERS,
TED ROGERS
AND LIONEL BLAIR

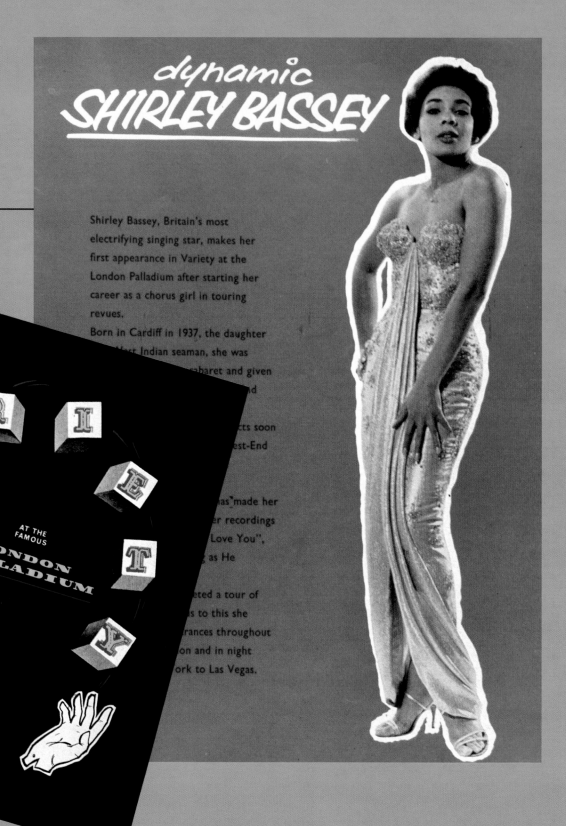

dynamic
SHIRLEY BASSEY

Shirley Bassey, Britain's most
electrifying singing star, makes her
first appearance in Variety at the
London Palladium after starting her
career as a chorus girl in touring
revues.

Born in Cardiff in 1937, the daughter
of a West Indian seaman, she was
discovered in cabaret and given
her first break in the show *Such Is
Life*. Her acts soon
appeared in the West-End

She has made her
first recordings
"As I Love You",
and sang as He

completed a tour of
Australia. In addition to this she
made appearances throughout
London and in night
clubs from New York to Las Vegas.

AT THE
FAMOUS
LONDON
PALLADIUM

PROGRAMME ONE SHILLING

COLUMBIA

SHIRLEY BASSEY WITH NELSON RIDDLE AND HIS ORCHESTRA

stereo

SHIRLEY BASSEY

mono

COLUMBIA

SHIRLEY BASSEY

On Record

LOVE IS A MANY SPLENDORED THING
THE NEARNESS OF YOU
FOOLS RUSH IN
WHO ARE WE?
ANGEL EYES
TILL
A LOVELY WAY TO SPEND AN EVENING
THIS LOVE OF MINE
YOU'RE NEARER
GOODBYE LOVER — HELLO FRIEND
WHERE OR WHEN
WHERE ARE YOU?
CLIMB EV'RY MOUNTAIN

"A heavenly body appearing as a luminous point . . . having an influence over a person's life" is the dictionary definition of the word 'star'. The legions of Shirley Bassey admirers are not likely to challenge this description. Shirley is an undoubted and undisputed star, and rightly enjoys an incomparable status. She stands outside and above any ordinary category of 'pop' singer, projecting her instinctive and dynamic talent on her own terms.

She possesses provocative beauty, intelligence, and abundant personal magnetism, and discharges it all with cross shots of fire and casual elegance which make her an electrifying stage presence, and a peerless recording artist.

She opens the first side with an exultant performance of the Webster/Fain *Love Is A Many Splendored Thing*, which is probably one of the most perceptive and impassioned interpretations ever given of this beautiful song; throughout this record it is her original and distinctive approach which emphasises Shirley Bassey's versatility, and her easy supremacy over her colleagues. Another highlight on this side is the wealth of estrangement and loss which she extracts from the lovely *Angel Eyes*—moods in which Geoff Love supports her admirably.

The second side sustains, and sometimes exceeds, the high level of the first. Starting with *A Lovely Way To Spend An Evening*, she purrs, caresses and lilts her way through *This Love Of Mine* and *You're Nearer*, and reaches a thrilling peak in the haunting Newell/ Carr *Goodbye Lover — Hello Friend*. This is one of the loveliest compositions in the history of modern popular songs, with its pure melody and the heartbreaking understatement of its lyric—and Shirley handles it with love and finesse.

The climax of the side is reached in the Rodgers/Hammerstein 11 hit, *Climb Ev'ry Mountain*, from their last hit, *Sound Of Music* with which Shirley finishes the record.

The backing of the Rita Williams Singers introduces a refreshing and stimulating texture to both sides of this disc.

The inspired choice of songs and the dexterity and refinement of their direction is designed to illuminate the range of Shirley's accomplishments—and she would be the first to agree that in Geoff Love she has found an arranger and accompanist of virtuoso qualities to match her own. Geoff displays his blade-sharp awareness of every change in Shirley's mood and style and helps to make this disc an outstanding achievement; it is a supreme example of "oneness" between Artist, Musical Director and Recording Producer, and ranks high among E.M.I. successes.

But, oh, it is Shirley—lithe, lilting, lovable Shirley—who, in this fusion of style, mood and performance, wins the triple crown.

Pauline Grant sleeve notes

1962

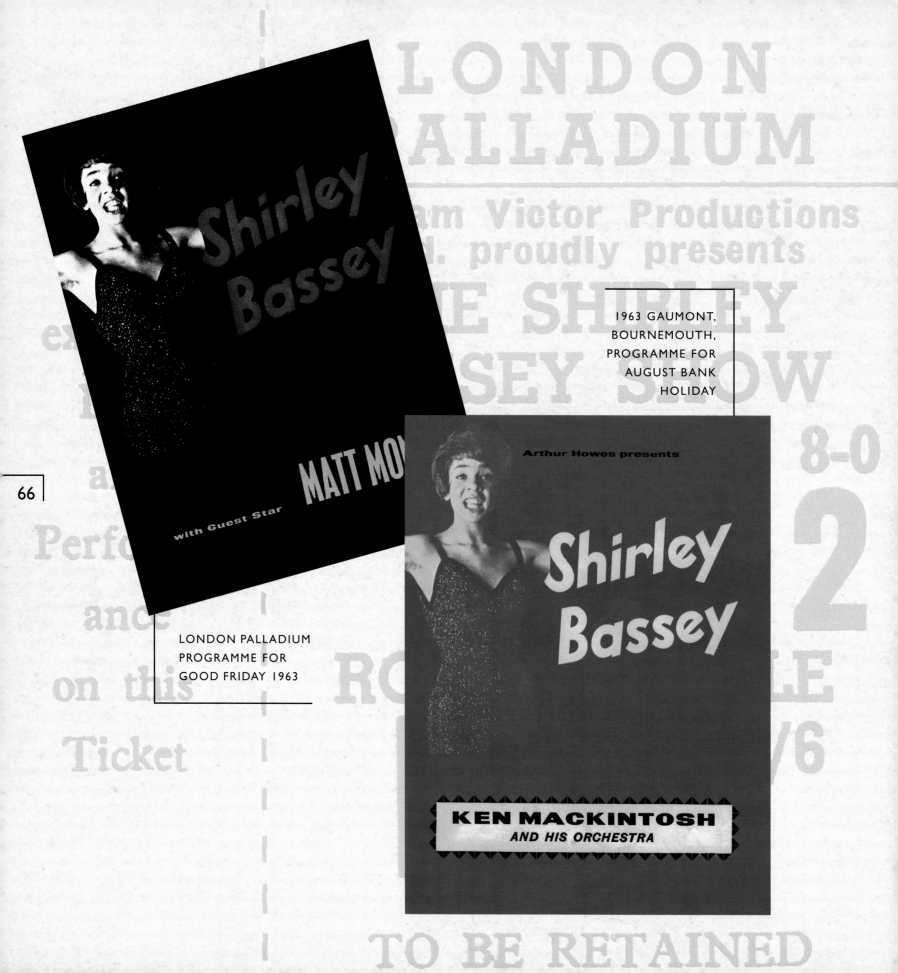

Shirley Bassey

with Guest Star

MATT MON

LONDON PALLADIUM
PROGRAMME FOR
GOOD FRIDAY 1963

1963 GAUMONT,
BOURNEMOUTH,
PROGRAMME FOR
AUGUST BANK
HOLIDAY

Arthur Howes presents

Shirley
Bassey

KEN MACKINTOSH
AND HIS ORCHESTRA

In Concert

PALLADIUM & TOUR

The London Palladium programme

was chosen from the titles below:-

WHAT KIND OF FOOL AM I

WHAT NOW MY LOVE

EVERYTHING IS COMING UP ROSES

THEY CAN'T TAKE THAT AWAY FROM ME

IN OTHER WORDS

GOODBYE LOVER

BIRTH OF THE BLUES

CLIMB EVERY MOUNTAIN

THE PARTY'S OVER

PLEASE MR. BROWN

AS LONG AS HE NEEDS ME

1963

SHIRLEY BASSEY
AT THE PIGALLE

stereo

IN PERSON

SHIRLEY BASSEY AT THE PIGALLE

A LOVELY WAY TO SPEND AN EVENING
ON A WONDERFUL DAY LIKE TODAY
I GET A KICK OUT OF YOU
WHO CAN I TURN TO?
YOU'D BETTER LOVE ME
THE OTHER WOMAN
HE LOVES ME
WITH THESE HANDS
A LOT OF LIVING TO DO
I (WHO HAVE NOTHING)
LA BAMBA
YOU CAN HAVE HIM
THE SECOND TIME AROUND
THE LADY IS A TRAMP
SOMEWHERE
ON A WONDERFUL DAY LIKE TODAY
A LOVELY WAY TO SPEND AN EVENING

AND THE CRITICS RAVED . . .

"BRAVO BASSEY. . . There are few artists who are capable of hynotizing a sophisticated night club audience. Usually the chatter of table companions and the clinking of champagne glasses are inevitable background noises to most cabaret acts. Shirley Bassey, however, who opened on Sunday for an eight weeks season at the Pigalle is one of those artists who cuts through the fidgeting like a knife and compels attention. She had her audience completely under her spell from the moment she opened her act singing *Wonderful Day Like Today* . . . Here was the late Edith Piaf, the fabulous Lena Horne, Garland, plus all the greats of yesterday rolled into one."

Peter Hepple . . . The Stage

"SHIRLEY SHINES . . . Shirley shines in cabaret. I look forward to seeing if this time a record can do her justice."

John Wells... Musical Express, London

"SHIRLEY'S TRIUMPH . . . Triumphant—that's the only word to describe Shirley Bassey's cabaret opening at the Pigalle, Piccadilly Circus, on Sunday."

T.G... Record Mirror, London

"SHIRLEY . . . For she was sensational. Today, she must be Britain's number one cabaret attraction. Her singing is more assured, her performance more polished, her delivery timed to perfection, her appearance—wow!"

J. H... Melody Maker, London

"BASSEY TURNS THE POWER ON . . . Hers is a voice in the great tradition of song belters. Here in London this week is an artist of international class willing and able to sing her heart out . . . she has few equals either in Europe or America."

R.K.W... Evening Standard, London

"Miss Bassey's 45-minute solo performance is immaculately conceived and expertly executed. Fronting the Alyn Ainsworth orchestra onstage, she exudes personality and vivacity."

Myro . . . Variety, London

1965

People ask: "When was Shirley Bassey last in a West End theatre?" The answer is: "At the London Palladium in 1962", which leads naturally to another question: "Where has she been lately?" The answer here is so long, so greatly caught up in world travel and so non-stop that there isn't space to give it fully.

But, glancing through page after page of the Bassey engagement book, one thing becomes very plain: Miss Bassey hardly ever takes a holiday. Instead of a long bask on sun-drenched sands, now so much a part of big star life, Miss Bassey just seems to slip from 'plane to 'plane—Australia, the Philippines, the Middle East, America, New Zealand, most European countries—it's like flipping through the pages of a skyways guide to the world. And, of course, she has many engagements in this country as well—concerts, cabaret, TV, theatres. You name the place, and if it's big, packed and popular, Miss Bassey will have been there.

Last year Miss Bassey was in the Royal Variety Performance, then she toured clubs in the North, made a couple of TV appearances on Sunday Night at the London Palladium, did her own BBC TV show, *The Sounds of Shirley Bassey*, and was packed out with concerts and other dates in between.

In January, Miss Bassey flew to Australia and gave seven concerts in Melbourne. She was so successful that her season was extended. After that came a month in a Sydney theatre-restaurant, then dates in New Zealand, then back to Brisbane, then to Manila, then on to New York. Her total rest after this world travel was five days.

In April Miss Bassey cut her first single for United Artists—*Don't Take The Lovers From The World*. Just afterwards she was given a special gala opening of her season at the Royal Box, New York, with an audience packed with the big names of show business. They even flew the Welsh flag — a feather in the cap of Tiger Bay—over the place all through the season. And flew it again in Las Vegas when she went on for a season there.

After that, back to New York, where she recorded her LP *I've Got A Song For You*. About an hour after leaving the studio, Miss Bassey was in a 'plane for London and this show. After the Prince of Wales, she has a concert in Blackpool and then a gala performance in Cannes and another concert in Blackpool. They come in quick succession, the first of an apparently limitless string of engagements. A life of country to country by 'plane. Wonderful for those who can stand the pace, the excitement, the adulation . . . But singularly bereft of long, lazy, sparkling holidays. Yet Shirley thrives . . .

Strange now to look back on that Al Read Show at the Adelphi, where an unknown girl came on stage, and sang Ross Parker's song *Who's Got A Match worth Striking?*, and became famous overnight.

Prince of Wales programme notes

1966

BILL BOORNE'S late night SPOT

NEVER, in Shirley Bassey's many appearances in London—and I have seen them all—has she had such an hysterical and fantastic reception as came her way at the Prince of Wales Theatre last night. It had to be seen and heard to be believed.

Young men—the majority in dinner jackets—were her most enthusiastic admirers.

They didn't want to know about those on the bill who preceded her.

When, eventually, Miss Bassey did arrive, in a yellow coat with ostrich feather sleeves, the audience stood and applauded as though she were a world name from the States. She might never have been seen here before.

Every number she sang was applauded wildly.

And at the end of the show when Shirley's two children, Sharon and Samantha, were brought on, Shirley was so overcome that she ignored those who were to present her with flowers galore. And the audience in the stalls swept down towards the stage to yell their appreciation to the star.

What a night!

KENNETH HOME presents
SHIRLEY BASSEY ENTERTAINS

Prince of Wales Theatre

Playbill
PROGRAMME 1s

I'VE GOT A SONG FOR YOU
I'M GLAD THERE IS YOU
JOHNNY ONE NOTE
THE SHADOW OF YOUR SMILE
KISS ME HONEY, HONEY
YOU CAN HAVE HIM
YOU'RE GONNA HEAR FROM ME
ALL OR NOTHING AT ALL
SHIRLEY
STRANGERS IN THE NIGHT
LET ME SING - AND I'M HAPPY
THE SOUND OF MUSIC

ALBUM SHOWN IS THE
BRAZILIAN RELEASE OF
I'VE GOT A SONG FOR YOU

72

Each Shirley Bassey album is a complete entertainment in itself. In this case, the fabulous Miss Bassey takes twelve contrasting songs and moulds each one into a memorable treatment. From the Frank Sinatra hit *Strangers In The Night* that started life in a film called *A Man Could Get Killed* to a song that the younger Sinatra sang with Harry James' Orchestra back in 1939, namely *All Or Nothing At All*; from standards by Andre and Dory Previn, Richard Rodgers, Lorenz Hart, Oscar Hammerstein and Irving Berlin to a newer version of *Kiss Me Honey, Honey*—a song Shirley recorded originally in 1959 and which became a landmark in her early career.

Brazilian sleeve notes

"I've got a song for you" says Shirley.

It was in Las Vegas in April this year that Shirley Bassey and manager Kenneth Hume decided to make this album. They wanted to show a new side of Shirley's talent and have deliberately included many up-tempo numbers along with the ballads.

Ralph Burns—American arranger famous for his orchestrations with the Woody Herman band and for top singers Lena Home, Sarah Vaughan, Johnny Mathis and Barbara Streisand, as well as for a score of Broadway musicals including *Funny Girl*—flew out to Las Vegas and prepared and rehearsed the numbers . . . no easy task for Shirley, who was doing two long shows a night, seven nights a week, at the Sahara Hotel.

As soon as the season closed they all flew to New York, to the studios of United Artists Records, and within one week had recorded this exciting new album.

United Artists Records in conjunction with Kenneth Hume worked non-stop to get this album ready for sale in time for the opening of Shirley Bassey's new show at the Prince of Wales Theatre, London on July 19th, 1966.

Programme notes

1966

SHIRLEY BASSEY

I'VE GOT A SONG
FOR YOU

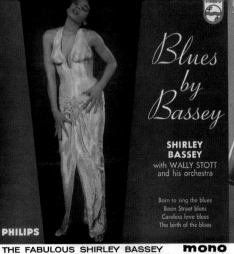

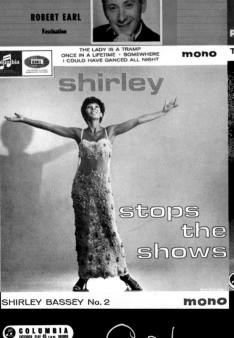

AND WE WERE LOVERS

AND WE WERE LOVERS
SUMMER WIND
SOMEBODY LIKE ME
IT MUST BE HIM (Seal Sur Son Etoile)
BIG SPENDER
THE IMPOSSIBLE DREAM
DOMMAGE, DOMMAGE (Too Bad, Too Bad)
ON A CLEAR DAY YOU CAN SEE FOREVER
IF YOU GO AWAY (Ne Me Quitte Pas)
THAT'S LIFE

Dear Shirley,

It's been a bang-bang day. Too much work. Too much work undone. An hour ago, the test pressing of your album arrived and I used it as an excuse to begin unwinding.

Maybe it's the scotch. Maybe it's the time of evening and the fact that I'm by myself—whatever, I am unwinding and next to me is that probing, prying voice of yours—now warm, now cold as an iceberg, coaxing out my song and a brilliant programme of other tunes.

Thank you for singing *If You Go Away*. Thank you for doing something different with it. Also, thank you for singing everything you sing. Most of all, thank you for being beautiful always and in all ways—and tonight, thanks for helping me to let go.

I love you,

Rod McKuen

Letter from Rod McKuen, who wrote the song *If You Go Away*.

1967

shirley bassey

and we were lovers

and we were lovers / summer wind
somebody like me / it must be him
big spender / the impossible dream
dommage, dommage (too bad, too bad)
on a clear day / that's life
if you go away (ne me quitte pas)

In Concert

UK AND USA CONCERT TOURS

bassey

WALDORF-ASTORIA

Week October 21, 1967

where

to go
what to do
when in New York

Exciting singing star Shirley Bassey casts her spell at the Empire Room of The Waldorf-Astoria twice each evening, Monday through Saturday. Dinner and supper are served and there is continuous dancing to two orchestras.

2/6

NEW YORK'S
WHERE TO GO
MAGAZINE

1967
TOUR PROGRAMME
COVER

1967

SHIRLEY BASSEY
THIS IS MY LIFE

GOING OUT OF MY HEAD
YOU GO TO MY HEAD

WHERE IS TOMORROW?
SOFTLY AS I LEAVE YOU
I MUST KNOW
A TIME FOR US
THIS IS MY LIFE
I'VE BEEN LOVED
NOW YOU WANT TO BE LOVED
SUNNY
FUNNY GIRL
WHO AM I?
THE JOKER

united artists

THIS *On Record* IS MY LIFE

NOW YOU WANT TO BE LOVED

Medley: *GOIN' OUT OF MY HEAD*

SOFTLY AS I LEAVE YOU

A TIME FOR US

THE JOKER

I MUST KNOW

THIS IS MY LIFE (La Vita)

WHO AM I?

FUNNY GIRL

SUNNY

I'VE BEEN LOVED

WHERE IS TOMORROW?

As she steps on stage and glides to the microphone the audience is immediately drawn to her in "moth to flame" fashion. She is dressed in a gown so dazzling that it seems to illuminate the entire room. In the background a group of musicians blend their collective talents into a song introduction. The audience leans forward, ever so slightly, and then the beautiful lady at the microphone begins to sing...

So begins a live performance by Shirley Bassey and by the time it's over both star and audience have been involved in more than a show; they have been involved in an experience: The star, because she has again presented tangible proof of her greatness... she has drawn from the deepest recesses of her ability to do more than entertain; she has actually lived her songs... the audience because they were the recipients of all this emotion and were given a rare opportunity to look into someone's soul.

The reasons for Shirley Bassey's ability to convey so much feeling to an audience are as varied and complex as the woman herself. She has, of course, had the practical experience that is essential to a great performer. Starting with club dates in her native Wales, Shirley eventually worked her way to England, Australia and America stopping shows all along the route. The scenes of her triumphs included the London Palladium, the Astor Club in London's equivalent of Broadway; the West End and the top niteries in New York, Las Vegas and Hollywood.

But most reasonably accomplished performers can stand before a group of people and entertain, what sets Shirley Bassey so far above them? It is her ability to relate to people, pure and simple.

When Shirley sings this album's title song you know this is her life.— When she sings of love, she is in love — When she belts out an upbeat number, she is happy and anyone within hearing range runs the gamut of emotions with her.

Shirley Bassey is one of the finest performers to electrify an audience in many years and she keeps getting better. So listen, and you'll know it's beautiful and true when Shirley Bassey says:

THIS IS MY LIFE.

1968

BROADWAY – BASSEY'S WAY

A LOT OF LIVIN' TO DO
PEOPLE
COME BACK TO ME
I'LL OVER ME
IF EVER I WOULD LEAVE YOU
I COULD HAVE DANCED ALL NIGHT
ONE OF THOSE SONGS
SOMETHING'S COMING
SOMETHING WONDERFUL
EVERYTHING'S COMING UP ROSES
BILL
THE IMPOSSIBLE DREAM
DON'T RAIN ON MY PARADE
I BELIEVE IN YOU
AND I LOVE I TURN TO

EMI
Columbia

GOLDEN HITS
OF SHIRLEY BASSEY

GOLDFINGER
(from film of same name)

I (Who Have Nothing)
(Uno dei tanti)

WHAT NOW MY LOVE
(Becaud · Sigman · Delance)

CLIMB EV'RY MOUNTAIN
(from „The Sound of Music„)

TILL (Danvers · Sigman)

THE PARTY'S OVER
(Styne · Green · Comden)

NO REGRETS (Dumont · Davis)

mfi

The Fabulous
Shirley
Bassey

IM IN THE MOOD FOR LOVE

Shirley Bassey

INCLUDING
THERE WILL NEVER
BE ANOTHER YOU
THE DAYS OF WINE
AND ROSES
I GET A KICK OUT
OF YOU
THE NEARNESS OF
YOU
I WISH YOU LOVE
WHAT NOW MY
LOVE
MOON RIVER
THE LIQUIDATOR
TONIGHT
PEOPLE

ORIGINAL MOTION PICTURE SOUNDTRACK

DEADFALL

COMPOSED & CONDUCTED BY
JOHN BARRY
"MY LOVE HAS TWO FACES" SUNG BY
SHIRLEY BASSEY
RENATA TARRAGO

SHIRLEY BASSEY
THIS IS MY LIFE

On K
ALBUMS

Shirley Bassey Collection

CALENDAR
RECORDS

SHIRLEY BASSEY

the
GOLDEN SOUND
of Shirley Bassey

12 ~~ONE~~ OF THOSE SONGS

Shirley Bassey

COME BACK TO ME
I'M A FOOL TO WANT YOU
A HOUSE IS NOT A HOME
IF LOVE WERE ALL
MOON RIVER
DON'T RAIN ON MY PARADE
SOMETHING'S COMING
DAYS OF WINE AND ROSES
CALL ME
CHARADE
I WISH YOU LOVE
ONE OF THOSE SONGS

A new collection of songs recorded by Shirley Bassey, like a new James Bond film, is an event.

Miss Bassey once honoured a film of mine by singing the title song of the picture—*Goldfinger*—and the song became a raging success in its own right. Now I can return the compliment by introducing this, the latest of her LPs. I certainly don't intend to sing—we can leave that to the quite overwhelming talent of Miss Bassey. But maybe I can say a few things about this album before you settle down to listen to it.

To generalise a bit, for openers, you can guarantee to hear every word of every song that Shirley sings. That, in itself is a bit of a novelty these days! There is a reason for this. The real Shirley Bassey comes through, clearly and unmistakably, in her songs. As she once told David Frost in a revealing interview (clad in an equally revealing gown) on television, she is able to explore and explain her many moods through the words and music of her songs in public far better than she ever could in private.

Every time I hear Shirley Bassey sing—and that includes the playing and re-playing of the same record—I am always thrilled and surprised by her extraordinary vocal range. There are notes on these tracks which catch at your heart by the very ease with which she reaches them. She seems to pluck them out of the air and hit them exactly, unerringly. You never have to worry in case she won't reach the high ones. She always does. When Shirley does a number it is hers, completely. Even if you have heard it before, sung by somebody else, she still seems to get an extra meaning, an extra dimension into the familiar words and out of the familiar tune. And when you next hear someone else sing it' you think "Ah, but you should hear what Shirley does with this". On this record you can.

No single album could completely capture ALL the many moods of the fantastic personality called Shirley Bassey, but in this collection, cunningly chosen by Shirley herself and produced by Norman Newell—the acknowledged master of his craft—you do get most: of them, from the brittle-bright to the softly lyrical; from the big brassy show business songs to the intimate numbers she is singing only for you—personally.

As for the individual numbers on this particularly well balanced bill, *Come Back To Me* is exciting as only Shirley Bassey can make a number exciting and thrilling. Then comes the dramatic *I'm A Fool To Want You* which is Bassey at her superb best. The mood changes in the wistful *A House Is Not A Home* before it comes to a song which could have been written for her—*If Love Were All*. We know that it comes from Noel Coward's *Bitter Sweet* and composed before she was even born, but it tells as few songs could of the inner heartaches of the gifted entertainer. Noel knew as if by some instinct what it is to have "a talent to amuse" and his song is re-born by her singing of it. *Moon River* is next and with it a fresh approach to a very familiar number. Shirley takes it both as a challenge and as an opportunity. Her approach, as in all her numbers, is personal. As a result, it is unique. Side one closes with the number which the bewitching Miss Bassey uses as her opener in her cabaret performances these days—*Don't Rain On My Parade* from the hit-show *Funny Girl*. It tells its own story from the inside and in it the girl never gets a breath wrong—she never does, even with the tricky cross-rhythms of *Something's Coming*, which opens Side Two with its variations of pace and its great feeling of latent power held surely in check as the voice and the orchestra balance, as if on a knife-edge of thrilling sounds. A great track this and one of my favourites. *Days Of Wine And Roses* gives us Shirley the Singer—so beautiful that it catches your breath. When I say "Shirley sings" I mean just that. Every shade of feeling, every ounce of meaning, all are suggested and expressed as in all her songs.

The next number is *Call Me*—warm and tender (like the song itself says), but with undertones of something more. Is it desperation, perhaps? Then *Charade*, a self-styled sad little serenade yet sung with power to give yet another apparent contradiction in the make-up of this amazing artiste—tantalising yet satisfying.

Shirley next sings *I Wish You Love* with a warmth and sincerity of feeling that she must surely feel in order to put it across so very beautifully, but you could say that about all these numbers and it would still be true. Finally *One Of Those Songs*, which gives this album its title is as exciting a number as one could wish for to close with.

Sean Connery sleeve notes

SHIRLEY BASSEY
does anybody miss me

WHO CAN I TURN TO
AS LONG AS HE NEEDS ME
GOLDFINGER
I (WHO HAVE NOTHING)
YOU'LL NEVER KNOW
WHAT NOW MY LOVE
WHAT KIND OF FOOL AM I
CLIMB EV'RY MOUNTAIN
TILL
REACH FOR THE STARS
THE PARTY'S OVER
ONCE IN A LIFETIME
WITH THESE HANDS
NO REGRETS

DOES ANYBODY MISS ME
I'LL NEVER FALL IN LOVE AGAIN
NEVER, NEVER NO
PICTURE PUZZLE
I ONLY MISS HIM
AS I LOVE YOU
I THINK OF ME
(YOU ARE) MY WAY OF LIFE
WE
GIVE ME YOU
IT'S ALWAYS 4A.M
HOLD ME, THRILL ME, KISS ME

1968/9

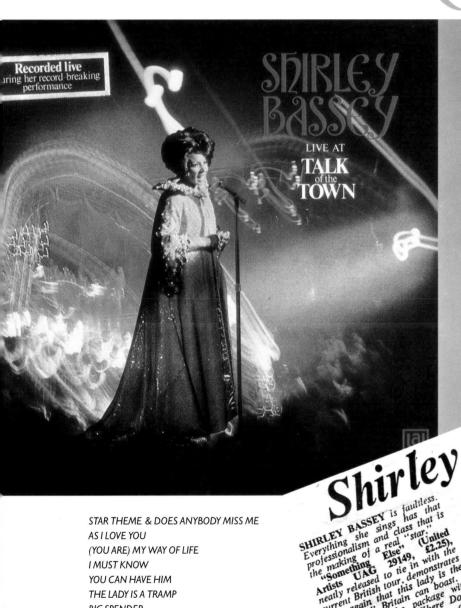

Recorded live
during her record-breaking
performance

SHIRLEY BASSEY

LIVE AT
TALK of the TOWN

Shirley Bassey

something else

Including
(WHERE DO I BEGIN) LOVE STORY
IT'S IMPOSSIBLE
BRIDGE OVER TROUBLED WATER
PIECES OF DREAMS
UNTIL IT'S TIME FOR YOU TO GO
TILL LOVE TOUCHES YOUR LIFE

STAR THEME & DOES ANYBODY MISS ME
AS I LOVE YOU
(YOU ARE) MY WAY OF LIFE
I MUST KNOW
YOU CAN HAVE HIM
THE LADY IS A TRAMP
BIG SPENDER
I'LL NEVER FALL IN LOVE AGAIN
THE JOKER
FUNNY GIRL
YOU AND I
THIS IS MY LIFE (LA VITA) & STAR THEME

Shirley still shining

SHIRLEY BASSEY is faultless. Everything she sings has that professionalism and class that is the making of a real "star."

"Something Else", (United Artists UAG 29149, £2.25), neatly released to tie in with the current British tour, demonstrates once again that this lady is the only "star" Britain can boast.

She opens the package with her latest single "(Where Do I Begin) Love Story." She also includes two other film themes, "Pieces Of Dreams" and "Till Love Touches Your Life," and also does versions of "It's Impossible" and "Bridge Over Troubled Water." There's also

a very suggestive version of "Breakfast In Bed" and "Excuse Me," a great little song, which deserves to be heard more of. Miss Bassey really expresses that one favourite track. Apparently it's also her favourite track.

Like the last, the album's produced, arranged and conducted by Johnny Harris, who seems to be the ideal collaborator and it's going to be another huge seller.

(WHERE DO I BEGIN) LOVE STORY
TILL LOVE TOUCHES YOUR LIFE
EASY THING TO DO
UNTIL IT'S TIME FOR YOU TO GO
IT'S IMPOSSIBLE
WHAT'S DONE IS DONE
PIECES OF DREAMS
BREAKFAST IN BED
EXCUSE ME
BRIDGE OVER TROUBLED WATERS
I'M NOT THERE
I'D LIKE TO HATE MYSELF IN THE MORNING

1970/1

I like the challenge of trying a song that nobody expects me to do - for instance, the Foreigner song 'I Want To Know What Love Is'. Nobody expected me to do that. Or the Beatles' song 'Something'. When I first sang it everybody said, 'Oh, no, no, no.' Then, when I wanted to record it, they said, 'No, no, no, it's a Beatles song, it's a group song.' And the more they told me not to do it the more I wanted to. And when I did it I proved them wrong, because it was number four in England for me.

At the very beginning there was always somebody choosing my material and I didn't feel right with an awful lot of it. So when my manager used to tell me that I was going to be a big star one day, I thought in the back of my mind that if I ever became a star the first thing would be that nobody would choose material for me. I'd choose it, I decided. And that's what has happened: I choose the material, and I really enjoy it. Putting the act together is sometimes very difficult, because it's like writing a story. You have to find the beginning, the middle and the end. I start off by searching for the opening song. Once I've found that, the second number comes easier and the third one and so on. But then I sometimes get stuck in the middle. And when I find the middle song, I just carry on. Then I get stuck for the final number. And eventually I find the right closing song too.

I don't always recognize the right songs for me the first time I hear them. For a long time I was asked to do 'Johnny One Note', but I couldn't do it for many, many years. Then one day Eddie Fisher's musical director just sat at the piano and said, 'This is a good song for you', and started playing 'Johnny One Note'. The way he played it, I got so excited, but I said, 'I can't do this song.' 'Why not?' he asked. 'Well, when I was discovered, the girl whose place I took in the show, she had a big hit with this song and I've never been able to touch this song.' 'Well, try it,' he said. And I was amazed when I opened my mouth: this voice came out singing this song as though it was mine. So, after all those years - it was about ten years, I believe - when we actually got down to it, it was a piece of cake.

I'm often asked about the Bond songs. Did I find them or did they find me? Actually 'Goldfinger' found me. John Barry wrote the music. We were touring England at the time and he was conducting for me. One day he said, 'There is this new song for the James Bond film Goldfinger and we'd like you to do it. I know your rule that you will never listen to a song unless there are words. There are no words, I must warn you - there's only the music, which I have done. And we're waiting on the lyric.' And because we had such a wonderful relationship on our tour I said to John, 'Well, I'll listen to it. I'll break my rule.' And thank God I did, because the moment he played the music to me, I got goose pimples, and I told him, 'I don't care what the words are. I'll do it.' And fortunately the words - they were by Tim Eury and Lesley Bricusse - were great.

Sinatra always used to say that picking material was the absolute cornerstone of building a sophisticated act, and as you build a relationship with the audience you get identified with those songs. I've learnt over the years that you have to sing songs that the audience can identify with. In the very beginning, before I had any hit records, I chose songs that were sung by other people, other people's hits. So when I did go out on stage and sang these songs, the audience knew them. But that was before I built up my own repertoire, and I believe it's so important to find the songs for your own voice. Which takes me back to when I first started to record and everybody was giving me this song and that song and it wasn't me, because I hadn't chosen them. I didn't feel them. Some I did, but a lot I didn't. It's so important to believe in a song, because when you do, then you can sell it to the audience and they will believe in it too.

Then again, there's always that one song that you think is great and you put it into the act, but maybe you put it in the wrong place and it doesn't go well because of the number that has come before it. I've found that at times, so I've switched the song around, put it somewhere else, and it has worked.

With songs, it's like telling a story. In a way you must pick the song to follow the one before, and then build and build and build, but then you must eventually come down, because you can't keep taking the audience up and up and up. You have to take the audience with you, like riding waves. You take them up, and then you bring them down a little, then you take them back up a little.

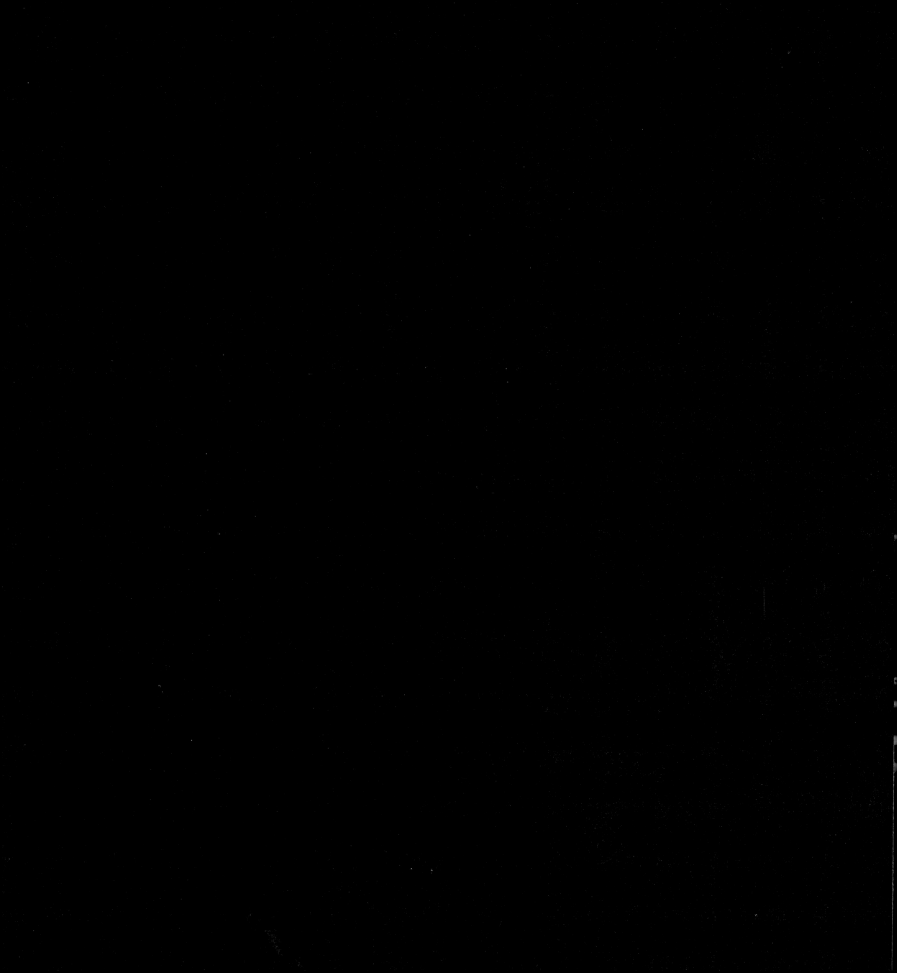

B A *Shirley* S E Y

Diamonds Are Forever

SOMETHING

SOMETHING
SPINNING WHEEL
YESTERDAY I HEARD THE RAIN
SEA AND SAND
MY WAY
WHAT ABOUT TODAY?
YOU AND I
LIGHT MY FIRE
EASY TO BE HARD
LIFE GOES ON
WHAT ARE YOU DOING THE REST OF YOUR LIFE?
YESTERDAY WHEN I WAS YOUNG

Shirley Bassey is really "Something" is more than a wolf-whistle observation, a spicy compliment, a stimulating utterance.

It is an expression of happiness voiced with intensity, with passion, with an urge to stir. It is a high-voltage performance and a lo-and-behold-en bow to the music of the day. It is an emotional climate. Warm. Whetting romantic appetite. Shadow and contrast. It is something else.

Shirley Bassey is something else. When she sings you can sense the titillation of an exotic tough. Her voice gently scratches your back, raising bumper crops of erotic imaginings. Then her gusto and enthusiasms jet you into a quick-developing sense of joy bubbling over. When Shirley sings she is saying something.

Have you ever seen Shirley perform? She undulates across a world of make-believe with a wink in her walk. She strips away the sham of trivial gimmickry in putting forth her particular thoughts. She sings with body English, controlling the exterior flamboyance, concentrating on the ear-soothing essentials. Shirley gets to you.

The selections here are really something. Traditions of today, transmitting ideas and conclusions, uplifts and down-drafted recollections, outlooks and inner transformations. The variety of choice runs across the entire spectrum of generations. Look at the timeless list. A song of The Beatles and of The Doors. A moving moment from the robust *Hair*. The beautiful Academy-Award-nominee *What Are You Doing The Rest Of Your Life?*" by Michel Legrand and the Bergmans. Songs from Blood, Sweat And Tears and Barbra Streisand. It adds up to a dozen delighting interpretations.

Shirley Bassey is contemporary. And a traditionalist. She wants to get the facts of the message she is singing straight. She wants you to get the facts straight. Thus she choreographs her presentments, toe-dancing on the top of a note, underscoring the highpoint of meaning. She half hugs the melody as she strides across a lyric line, a tiger at bay, a tender pussycat.

She seems to be seeing inside the words and unfolding them for your viewing pleasure. She looks upon it all through wide-angle lenses, boldly snapping up-to-date photos of the world around us. She enunciates her position with perfect clarity. She is no screaming expressionist, no eek-freak screeching to a halting conclusion. Shirley is understandable.

Shirley Bassey is really "Something" is really something. It is a spray of love potion to curl you up in a blanket. It is a long, lingering look at the music scene today. It is a statement of fact about Shirley. She lurks behind each sly thought. She urges you on with her rapt interest. She is satisfying.

"Shirley Bassey Is Really Something"—else!

Mort Goode American sleeve notes

93

1970

In Concert

B R I T I S H   T O U R

ROYAL FESTIVAL HALL
GENERAL MANAGER: JOHN DENISON, C.B.

SHIRLEY BASSEY

with BRIAN FAHEY & his Orchest

FRIDAY, 6 NOVEMBER, 197

6.15 p.m.

Management: International Light Entertainment Ltd

STALLS

£2·50   50/-

GANGWAY 2
ROW   SEAT
E   8

1970

GREEN

SIDE

AT NINE THIRTY   'BERNARD DELFONT'   AT ELEVEN O'CLOCK
PRESENTS
'ROBERT NESBITT'S
diamond
studded REVue   in the star spot

JET SET 70

STAGED & CHOREOGRAPHED BY   PRODUCED BY   BOOK BY
BILLY PETCH   ST. JOHN ROPER TOD KINGMAN
ORCHESTRATIONS BY BURT RHODES   MUSIC BY RON GRAINER

THE SUPER 70's — THE JET AGE ★ ★ ★ ★   DANCING TO
A Man on the Move: MICHAEL ROWLATT   THE MUSIC OF:
Two Birds on the Wing: ZENA CLIFTON · PAULA LANE
The Jet Setters: LINDA DUNN, BOBBY HANNA, BRENDA MAY, JIMMY ANTHONY   The PHIL PHILLIPS
A Cosmopolitan Lady: DIANA QUISEEKAY   GROUP
'JET SET TAKE OFF ★ ★ ★ ★ · 'LET GO'
'BONJOUR PARIS' — VIVE LA CONCORDE ★ ★ ★ ★   FRANK DENIZ
MICHAEL ROWLATT and LES GIRLS   LATIN RHYTHMS
'BOUZOUKI NIGHTS' — MUSIQUE À LA GRECQUE ★ ★ ★ ★
BRENDA MAY and the 'AEGEAN GYPSIES'   BURT RHODES
Il Capitano: MICHAEL ROWLATT   AND HIS
The Pearl of Piraeus: DIANA QUISEEKAY   ORCHESTRA
Her Admirers: GEORGE NICHOL, JOHN FROST, STEVE CORNELL, ERIC WILSON
('The Spirit of Greece' written and composed by James Gilbert)
'VIVA LAS VEGAS' — DESERT TOUCH DOWN ★ ★ ★ ★
PAULA LANE and THE MIDNIGHT COWBOYS and GIRLS
The Gunslinger: BOBBY HANNA, JIMMY ANTHONY
CONTINENTAL CARNIVAL — LES NUITS DE GALA ★ ★ ★ ★
MICHAEL ROWLATT, DIANA QUISEEKAY and REVELLERS
Les Belles Masquées: ZENA CLIFTON, PAULA LANE
PALAZZO PARTY — VENISE EN FÊTE ★ ★ ★ ★
THE ENTIRE COMPANY ★ ★ ★ ★

SHIRLEY BASSEY

Musical Director: BRIAN FAHEY

Miss Bassey's gowns by: DOUGLAS DARNELL

Emotive Bassey

EVERYBODY has missed Shirley Bassey since her last tour, and there was no need for her to ask if they had. But she did, and was given the tremendous response she deserved at Leicester's De Montfort Hall at the opening of her tour on Sunday

The reason she is one of the world's top performers is because her whole approach is that of the professional. On every number she becomes emotionally involved and lets her feelings flow freely.

She swings with the up-tempo songs such as "The Lady Is A Tramp," or "Light My Fire," her hips constantly swaying provocatively. Yet on the ballads she sings with sincerity and conviction, reliving an experience — or so it seems. All the time her body works with the music emphasising its strength.

Miss Bassey's voice is an instrument; sometimes mellow with a silky smoothness depending on the mood, or when she has " her motor running," earthy, tantalising and powerful. But her whole performance is enhanced by Brian Fahey and his orchestra.

She sings for the people and included her most memorable numbers, " Big Spender," " I Who Have Nothing," " Someth___" and " As I Love You," plus th__ " It's Impossible."
McNALLY.

SHIRLEY BASSEY: Portsmouth (23); Bournemouth ___ns (24); Royal Albert (25); Newcastle City

___SDAY, APRIL 22, 1971

ROYAL ALBERT HALL
General Manager: FRANK J. MUNDY

Sunday, 25 April, 1971

At 9 p.m   Doors open at 8.30

ROBERT PATERSON presents
SHIRLEY BASSEY

| ARENA | **A** | £2.50 | 50/- |

ROW **2**

SEAT **10**

Enter by Door No. **2**

TO BE RETAINED

ALBERT HALL this Su__

SHIRLEY

FEW RETURNED TICKETS & ST__
available on personal application only.

NOVEMBER 21 SUNDA

The Royal Variety Performance

In the presence of Her Majesty the Queen
Tonight at 7.55

SHIRLEY BASSEY
NORMAN COLLIER
TOMMY COOPER
DAILEY AND WAYNE
SACHA DISTEL
KEN GOODWIN

STEPHANE GRAPPELLI
HUGHIE GREEN
SID JAMES
THE LITTLE ANGELS
OF KOREA
THE NEW DOLLYS
THE NEW SEEKERS

JACK PARNELL
AND HIS ORCHESTRA
THE STUPIDS
THE VILLANS
LOVELACE WATKINS
THE YOUNG
GENERATION

THE LONDON PALLADIUM ORCHESTRA (under the direction of Robert Lowe)

Sacha Distel   Bruce Forsyth   Tommy Cooper   Hughie Green

Stephane Grappelli   Ken Goodwin   Shirley Bassey   Lovelace Watkins   Dailey and Wayne   Sid James

PRESENTED BY BERNARD DELFONT AT THE LONDON PALLADIUM, NOVEMBER 15, 1971
(IN AID OF THE VARIETY ARTISTES' BENEVOLENT FUND: ORGANISING SECRETARY REG
SWINSON, M.B.E.): THE SHOW STAGED BY ROBERT NESBITT: TELEVISION DIRECTION ALBERT
LOCKE: EXECUTIVE PRODUCER BILL WARD, O.B.E.
ATV Network Production

In Concert

B R I T I S H   T O U R - A P R I L   M A Y

Dear Hilary,

Thank you ... 1st.

I am glad to hear that you enjoyed my show at the Albert Hall, it was a memorable experience for me too, all those thousands of people cheering and cheering me, it ... difficult to express what I ... simply fantastic.

... your photograph signed.

... in England during November ... ill be appearing at the Ba ... Club ...

Kin ...

Shirley is one of the world's most travelled artists. Outside the U.K. she is in enormous demand throughout Europe where she works extensively every year in major festivals and Television shows. At the beginning of 1970, Shirley appeared at the main Gala of Midem, and at Bal Pare, the big television Gala of the Year in Germany. In March, she made one of her many trips to the States where she appeared in cabaret at the Shoreham Hotel in Washington D.C., and then went on to the Caribe Hilton in San Juan, Puerto Rico.

April of this year saw Shirley's return to the United Kingdom for the first time in two years, when she performed a two week session at "The Talk Of The Town" Her appearance broke all previous records of attendance.

In May and June, Shirley made her yearly visit to Australia and New Zealand, where she is enormously popular and the country's major recording artist. During her visit, she was presented with a gold disc for her album *And We Were Lovers*. This was the first gold disc awarded to a female recording artist in Australia.

In June, Shirley returned to London to record her one hour BBC 1 Television Special which was transmitted on August 13th. Before returning to the U.K. for this tour Shirley performed a cabaret season in September at the Sahara Hotel in Las Vegas, and in October at the Empire Room in the Waldorf Astoria Hotel, New York, where she received outstanding reviews.

Programme notes

CONCERT
TOUR
PROGRAMME
COVER

Yours sincerely,

Shirley Bassey

1971

I CAPRICORN

I CAPRICORN
THE LOOK OF LOVE
THE WAY A WOMAN LOVES
LOVE
WHERE AM I GOING
I'VE NEVER BEEN A WOMAN BEFORE
FOR ALL WE KNOW
THE GREATEST PERFORMANCE OF MY LIFE
WHERE IS LOVE
LOSING MY MIND
ONE LESS BELL TO ANSWER
LOST AND LONELY

SHIRLEY BASSEY

HUS 061

YO, CAPRICORNIO

1972

SOMEDAY
BLESS THE BEASTS AND CHILDREN
JEZAHEL
AND I LOVE YOU SO
THE WAY OF LOVE
THE FIRST TIME EVER I SAW YOUR FACE
DAY BY DAY
WITHOUT YOU
BALLAD OF THE SAD YOUNG MEN
I DON'T KNOW HOW TO LOVE HIM
I'D DO IT ALL AGAIN
IF WE ONLY HAVE LOVE

101

1972

SHIRLEY BASSEY COMPLETES TWELVE CITY TOUR – BROKEN BOX OFFICE RECORDS, STANDING OVATIONS

United Artists Records' international singing star, Shirley Bassey, completed a twelve city U.S.A. concert tour Sunday night (April 2nd) in Los Angeles, an itinerary which has proved to be one of the most successful personal appearance schedules ever undertaken by a UA artist.

A completely packed house at the Dorothy Chandler Pavillion of Los Angeles' famed Music Center gave Miss Bassey a long series of cheering, standing ovations to conclude her American trek which included box office and artistic triumphs in Baltimore, Philadelphia, New York, Louisville, Toledo, Chicago, Columbus, Toronto, Dallas, Houston, and Buffalo, in addition to Los Angeles.

At Lincoln Center in New York, Shirley engendered the largest non-benefit gross in the history of the august institution.

UA reports a great upsweep in sales of her current LP, *I Capricorn*, after each stop of Miss Bassey's itinerary Shirley Bassey returned to England on Monday, April 3rd, for personal appearances in Britain and the continent and additional recording sessions.

Press release

THIS IS YOUR LIFE

SHIRLEY BASSEY

"DON'T DO THIS TO ME" WERE MY WORDS WHEN EAMONN ANDREWS SURPRISED ME FOR THE *THIS IS YOUR LIFE* TV SHOW

1972

1972
DUTCH
CONCERT
PROGRAMME

1972
UK CONCERT
PROGRAMME

103

Shirley Bassey
Live at Carnegie Hall

Featuring Woody Herman and the Young Thundering Herd

LIVE AT CARNEGIE HALL

GOLDFINGER   WHERE AM I GOING   I CAPRICORN   LET ME SING AND I'M HAPPY   JOHNNY ONE NOTE   FOR ALL WE KNOW   I'D LIKE TO HATE MYSELF IN THE MORNING   I WHO HAVE NOTHING   DAY BY DAY   AND I LOVE YOU SO   DIAMONDS ARE FOREVER   BIG SPENDER   NEVER, NEVER, NEVER   YOU AND I   SOMETHING   THIS IS MY LIFE   THE PARTY'S OVER

When Shirley Bassey signed with United Artists in the mid 60's, she was already an established star in British show business. With many successful records to her credit such as *Kiss Me, Honey Honey, Kiss Me, As I Love You, I (Who Have Nothing), Faraway*, and *The Party's Over* . . . songs she is still asked to sing wherever she appears . . . they still sell in very large quantities on re-issue albums year after year to the joy of Shirley, who finds the continued sales appeal of these records a satisfying sign of loyalty from her fans of her earlier work.

When in 1969 Shirley took up residence in Switzerland she was unable to work in the UK for a period of two years and it was during this time that she recorded most of her songs in Los Angeles and produced the albums *Does Anybody Miss Me* and *This Is My Life*.

During her exile and living so close to Italy, I was able to convince Shirley that she should appear at the then "internationally-famous San Remo Festival. She was entered to sing *This Is My Life* and on the night she appeared, it was a landmark in her career in many ways, for she was acclaimed by the International audience, and the Italian public had discovered a new star. *This is My Life* did not however go through to the finals and the Italian Press conducted a campaign, voicing their objection to what they called the rejection of the greatest performer to appear at the Festival.

Since then I have been present at Shirley Bassey's performances in many parts of the world but San Remo remains for me the most nostalgically exciting performance of Shirley's I have ever seen.

This introduction to Italian audiences was followed by Ganzonissima (Italian road shows) tours, television spectaculars and concerts, which served to heighten her popularity with the Italian public. During this time, Shirley continued to play the most important cabaret, club and hotel engagements in Australia, New Zealand, Las Vegas, New York, Puerto Rico and Scandinavia. By this time she was able and ready to come back home to work and record in London after a two-year break.

It was then that Mike Stewart, President of United Artists, asked me to act as executive producer for Shirley's recordings - a task that was exciting but at the same time daunting when I realised all that had gone before over future recording plans with Shirley we decided to try a completely new approach to recording for her return to the London studios. Johnny Harris was engaged as arranger and producer and we had Shirley singing with a group known as Heads, Hands & Feet (soon to become known in the States in their own right) and this in itself was a departure, giving us more time to experiment with ideas in the treatment of songs and a good basis on which to build the arrangements around the vocal and rhythm tracks. This formula we have used since, and has proved to be immensely successful. The first album of this new era was called *Something* and of course included the title song written by George Harrison which went on to become another major world-wide hit single for Shirley. The next album was *Something Else* and is probably my personal favourite to this day and then followed *I Capricorn, And I Love You So* and her last studio LP *Never, Never, Never*. The latter set was named after the single of the same name, which was Shirley's personal choice and which became her biggest hit in the US since *Goldfinger*.

The second and most comprehensive Shirley Bassey tour of the United States started in April, 1973 including two sell out evenings at the renowned Carnegie Hall during which this exciting album was recorded. Here the reception at both shows was phenomenal with standing ovations even before she sang a note and the atmosphere has been faithfully captured here. I suppose you could call this a definitive record of Shirley Bassey's established repertoire with the added excitement of being there on the night... In other words, this is her life.

Noel Rogers sleeve notes

1973

108

AT THE
ROYAL
ALBERT
HALL

In Concert

S H I R L E Y   B A S S E Y

RECEIVING
TEN GOLD
DISCS FROM
DAVID FROST
AT THE
ROYAL
ALBERT
HALL

TVTIMES TOP 10 STAR PORTRAIT
SHIRLEY BASSEY

Readers of
TV Times
voted Shirley
Bassey the
Most Exciting
Female Singer
on TV of 1973.
Here,
ALAN
BRIEN
studies the
girl from
Tiger Bay . . .

1973
TV TIMES
FEATURE
PAGE

ROYAL ALBERT HALL
General Manager : ANTHONY J. CHARLTON

Friday 11 October 1974
at 9.15 p.m.   Doors open at 8.45
Robert Paterson presents
SHIRLEY BASSEY
in Concert

ROYAL
ALBERT
HALL
11 Oct
£4.00

ARENA

A
ROW 1

£4.00
Enter by
Door No. 2

Arena

A
1 ROW

SEAT 1
TO BE RETAINED   SEE REVERSE

1 SEAT
TO BE GIVEN UP

1974 CONCERT
TOUR PROGRAMME

1973/4

NEVER, NEVER, NEVER   NOBODY DOES IT LIKE ME

NEVER, NEVER, NEVER
BABY I'M-A WANT YOU
SOMEONE WHO CARES
THE OLD FASHIONED WAY
I WON'T LAST A DAY WITHOUT YOU
SOMEHOW
THERE IS NO SUCH THING AS LOVE
KILLING ME SOFTLY WITH HIS SONG
GOING, GOING, GONE
NO REGRETS
TOGETHER
MAKE THE WORLD A LITTLE YOUNGER

LEAVE A LITTLE ROOM
WHEN YOU SMILE
ALL THAT LOVE WENT TO WASTE
DAVY
I'M NOT ANYONE
MORNING IN YOUR EYES
THE TROUBLE WITH HELLO IS GOODBYE
NOBODY DOES IT LIKE ME
I'M NOTHING WITHOUT YOU
YOU ARE THE SUNSHINE OF MY LIFE

1973/4

GOOD, BAD & BEAUTIFUL   **LOVE, LIFE & FEELINGS**

EMOTION	WHAT I DID FOR LOVE
SEND IN THE CLOWNS	THE HUNGRY YEARS
GOOD BAD BUT BEAUTIFUL	BORN TO LOSE
SING	EVERYTHING THAT TOUCHES YOU
THE WAY WE WERE	ISN'T IT A SHAME
I'LL BE YOUR AUDIENCE	MIDNIGHT BLUE
FEEL LIKE MAKIN' LOVE	THE WAY I WANT TO TOUCH YOU
ALL IN LOVE IS FAIR	NATALI
RUN ON AND ON AND ON	YOU'VE MADE ME SO VERY HAPPY
THE OTHER SIDE OF ME	ALONE AGAIN (NATURALLY)
JESSE	FEELINGS
LIVING	IF I NEVER SING ANOTHER SONG

1975/6

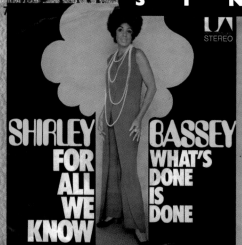

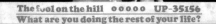

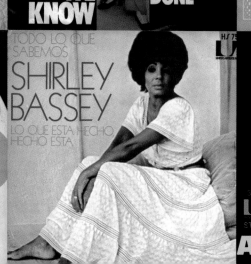

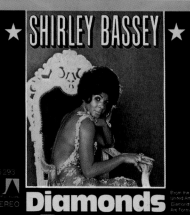

SMALL
SOUVENIR
PROGRAMME

AN EVENING WITH
SHIRLEY
BASSEY
Souvenir Programme
Fifty pence

Shirley Bassey

LONDON 30 October–5 November 1976 Price 11p
BBC Radio London: page 79

RadioTimes

Bassey's magic

Shirley Bassey sings
in a new six-part series
– her first for BBC1
– on Saturday nights.
Inside: Shirley's steps to stardom

RADIO
TIMES
FRONT
COVER

8.15 Shirley Bassey
making for BBC Television the
first series in her outstanding
career. Tonight: Show 2
Guest stars
Rolf Harris, Janis Ian
The Brythoniad Male Voice Choir
and Emma
with THE SHIRLEY BASSEY DANCERS

Orchestra conducted by
ARTHUR GREENSLADE
Choreographer NIGEL LYTHGOE
Make-up JEAN SPEAK
Film cameraman PHIL MEHEUX
Film sound JOHN MURPHY
Designer VICTOR MEREDITH
Producer STEWART MORRIS

1976
LARGE
TOUR
BROCHURE
WITH
CUT-OUT
CIRCLE
COVER

1976

114

In the Spring of 1975, Miss Bassey gave her most comprehensive tour yet in the United States including five totally sold-out consecutive days at Carnegie Hall, which established an all time record for solo artists in that famous venue.

During her lifetime she has received twenty-five gold albums from all over the world including South Africa, but ironically her first ever from her own country was last year for *The Shirley Bassey Singles*. Even *Goldfinger* was a gold album in the United States, but not in this country and naturally it was an immense source of delight to Shirley that finally this honour was bestowed upon her in Britain.

Last October, and one really runs out of epithets when describing Shirley's success, she made a triumphant return to Japan, where she was literally accorded a state reception.

At the end of 1975, she toured Holland, Belgium and concluded her European tour with four concerts at the Theatre Champs-Elysees in Paris, leaving her just enough time to come back and record her much acclaimed Christmas special for BBC Television.

Only last month she gave her fourteenth tour of Australia, the country in which curiously she was accepted as a superstar before Great Britain, and for that reason Australia remains a territory very close to Shirley's heart.

We welcome her back with great love and pride during this, her twentieth anniversary year in showbusiness.

Programme Notes

PHOTO SEQUENCE FOR *LOVE, LIFE AND FEELINGS* ALBUM COVER

The best of
Shirley Bassey

THE
SASSY
MISS BASSEY

UA

SPOTLIGHT ON
DOUBLE VALUE!
2 LPs FOR THE PRICE OF 1

THE WONDERFUL
SHIRLEY BASSEY
with Geoff Love & his Orchestra
MFP 50041 STEREO
mfp

A foggy day in London Town
I've got you under my skin
Cry me a river · The party's over
They can't take that away from me
The man that got away
I've never been in love before
I'll remember April · Easy to love
April in Paris · 'S wonderful
No one ever tells you

SHIRLEY BASSEY
BIG SPENDER
THE IMPOSSIBLE DREAM · THAT'S LIFE · IT MUST BE HIM · SUMMER WIND
ON A CLEAR DAY YOU CAN SEE FOREVER
SUNSET

SHIRLEY BASSEY

GREAT PERFORMANCE

THE BEST O
LIBERTY
A
VALUE

SHIRLEY
BASSEY

ATTENTION!
Shirley Bassey

Including:
Stormy Weather
The Banana Boat Song
As I Love You

fontana
special

GEM
2枚組 ¥3,700
GEM 1025/26

SHIRLEY BASSEY
LIVE IN JAPAN

シャーリー・バッシー・ライヴ・イン・ジャパン

完全限定盤
カラーピンナップ付!!

UA

"Shirley Bassey is the world's greatest female entertainer" That eulogy contained within a review in the New York Post of one of her concerts is open to argument by those who would possibly award such an accolade to other well-known ladies of song, but it is indicative that this dynamic girl from Cardiff is now without question in the world class of artists. That's as high as an entertainer can aspire to go, and only a handful attain and retain the exalted status as Shirley has.

She possesses all the attributes of a real star. A striking, vivaciously beautiful appearance which has rendered her instantly recognisable to millions in every corner of the globe and brought inevitable difficulties in preserving some necessary degree of personal peace and privacy. Plus a startling, dramatically unique singing voice that compels attention and can never be mistaken as anybody else's.

Shirley is one of the few singers who lives and feels every line and every nuance of emotion in her songs, mesmerising her audience with the power and passion of her interpretation and leaving them as physically and emotionally drained as herself at the end. There is nothing artificial or contrived about the vehemence of her performance; it all comes straight from the heart, and that fact is patently and immediately obvious to all who watch and listen.

The depth and extent of her interpretative skills were moulded in the harsh crucible of personal experience. Shirley comes from ordinary working class circumstances, and has undergone a full share of heartache and tragedy in her earlier years. But she did not surrender or succumb to adversity; she fought back and triumphed over it with courage and resolution which add so much to her performing powers today.

Shirley first drew attention when she was singing locally in Wales at the age of sixteen, and her first appearance in London was in a revue called *Such Is Life* at the Astor Club. This provided her with a valuable West End shop window for her talent, and resulted in a recording contract and the memorable performances you can hear in this double album, the first of a long and distinguished string of record hits and a gateway to the entire world. Now, seventeen years later, that world is at her feet, gladly and willingly. New York, Melbourne, Hollywood, Tokyo, London, Munich - the concert halls are sold out within hours of tickets for her shows becoming available, and the demands for encores grow ever longer and more insistent. She copes with everything like the true professional she is.

This double album reveals the full potency of Shirley's singing style and magnetic personality. It includes her earliest hits such as *Banana Boat Song*, *As I Love You*, *Kiss Me, Honey Honey, Kiss Me*, *Hands Across The Sea* and *Puh-leeze Mr. Brown*, and her outstanding renditions of some of the best popular song standards exemplified by Cole Porter's *Night And Day*, *From This Moment On*, and *Love For Sale*, the Rodgers and Hart favourite *My Funny Valentine* and Harold Arlen's *Stormy Weather* and *Blues In The Night*. To revert to our initial point, perhaps not everyone will agree that Shirley Bassey is the world's greatest female entertainer, but no one will quarrel with the Los Angeles Sentinel when it stated that she is "one of the greatest singers in the world".

Nigel Hunter sleeve notes

1976

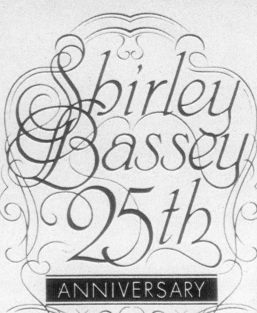

Shirley Bassey 25th ANNIVERSARY

In Concert

ROYAL ALBERT HALL
General Manager: ANTHONY J. CHARLTON
Monday, 20 March, 1978
at 9.15 p.m.   Doors open at 8.45
ROBERT PATERSON presents
SHIRLEY BASSEY
IN CONCERT

BALCONY   £3.50

ROW   **4**   Enter by
Door No. **8**

SEAT   **95**   SEE REVERSE

TO BE RETAINED   NO RE-ADMISSION

TICKET AND PHOTOS
FROM THE ROYAL ALBERT HALL

THE BEST OF PROMS Presents
The Proms Symphony Orchestra
and Choir conducted by Dirk Brossé
RANDY CRAWFORD
SHIRLEY BASSEY
16/10/93 · 20H · FLANDERS EXPO · GENT
02/773.66.77
MUSIC HALL · AVENUE DE TERVURENLAAN 166/4 · 1150 BRUSSELS
Knack   Het Volk

DUTCH
CONCERT
POSTER

Faces
The magazine about people
SHIRLEY BASSEY: LAST TOUR OF THE TIGRESS
The 'baby' out-starring Star Wars
Why Leslie Phillips is scared of marriage
Phil Drabble: One man and his dogs
WIN A COLOUR TV

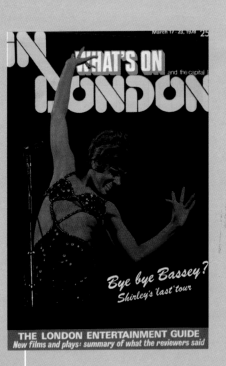

WHAT'S ON IN LONDON   and the capital
Bye bye Bassey?
Shirley's 'last' tour
THE LONDON ENTERTAINMENT GUIDE
New films and plays: summary of what the reviewers said

MAGAZINES FEATURING
EARLY RETIREMENT STORIES

1977/8

Shirley Bassey 25th

ANNIVERSARY

40 Greatest Hits

Including
As Long As He Needs Me
Kiss Me Honey, Honey Kiss Me
Climb Every Mountain, Big Spender
I (Who Have Nothing), As I Love You
Never Never Never, What Now My Love
Where Do I Begin, Something
For All We Know, Goldfinger

You can work it out on your fingers if you want to. Shirley Bassey made her first professional appearance in a touring revue called *Memories of Al Jolson* at the age of 16. This year Miss Bassey celebrates her silver jubilee in the business. Sixteen plus twenty five. Easy.

Only a few of them ever own up. But then, only a very few stay so young that it doesn't matter. Fewer still make that climb to the top and remain there long enough for us to bother with mental arithmetic at all. What is being celebrated really, then, is not statistics but stardom.

Stardom, film genius, is fairly easy to recognise but almost impossible to define. All we know is that it exists by public consent; when a sufficient number of the paying customers decide that a performer is a star, then he or she is a star, and that's that. In the beginning, Shirley Bassey didn't even want to become an entertainer, let alone a famous one, though entertainment has always been one of the recognised ways out of tough districts and drab streets. As the youngest of seven children in the dock area of Cardiff her first ambition was simply not to ha:ve to inherit any more cast-off clothing, so she dreamed of one day maybe working in a gown shop. "And I wanted to be a model; I wanted to be a nurse; I wanted to be so many things, almost anything but part of showbusiness. It wasn't one of those things when you're seven and you're watching the film your mother has taken you to and you say that's it, I'm going to be an actress or I'm going to be a singer. It never entered my head. Honestly."

She became someone special. In little more than two years after her entry into showbusiness she achieved what so few British artists ever achieve and that is to become a household name in the whole of Europe and, above all, America.

Acceptance in America was considerably helped by the enormous popularity of her record of the theme song of the James Bond film *Goldfinger* in 1964. But she had actually established herself there as early as 1961, in cabaret in New York. She was also a success in Las Vegas, which is vastly different from saying merely that she appeared there. Plenty of artists of very little standing appear in Las Vegas, for the place is greedy for entertainment. But the smaller acts work the smaller rooms, where the gamblers hardly stop betting long enough to notice. Shirley was not among the sideshows but in the big league. "I suppose I should feel hurt that I've never been really big in America on record since *Goldfinger*, and it's a pity in a way because the business in America is very much geared to the idea of a hit record. But, concertwise, I always sell out."

For the sake of completeness we can make a list of Shirley Bassey's achievements in the purely statistical sense - the 14 silver discs in Britain, Holland and France; and the 28 golds earned by sales in those countries and others as far apart as the South American States and Sweden. The TV Times named her Best Female Singer in 1972 and 1973; Music Week followed suit in 1974; in 1977 there was a Britannia Award for the Best Female Solo Singer in the Last 50 Years of Recorded Sound: the American Guild of Variety Artists voted her Best Female Entertainer for 1976; the late President John F. Kennedy invited her to sing at the White House. All that leaves out the various series of Carnegie Hall Concerts in 1972, 1973 and 1974, each lasting only a few evenings but which could probably have been extended to a couple of weeks and still sold out. It forgets her triumphant Paris debut as late as 1974 (British performers as a rule, don't make easy conquests in France). There have been four Royal Variety appearances and sell-out tours all over Europe. including the 22-day British tour in 1976 to mark her twenty years as a recording artist.

On her arrival in Britain earlier this year she had to announce her intention to semi-retire before the newspapers roused themselves. 'Semi-retirement' is simply an extension of a process already begun - a cutting down on the touring, an even greater choosiness in the selection of dates and venues, the spending of more time at home. Unlike Judy Garland, whom she understood so well and admired so much, she doesn't feel that she must have applause in order to feel alive. She has always accepted it and enjoyed it when it's been given, but it isn't part of her diet. The press is going to find it awfully dull, for singing to the delight of thousands of people, even only occasionally, is not news somehow. But it is and will continue to be to the audiences themselves, and they, after all, were the ones who started it, by noticing how extraordinary she was 25 years ago.

Peter Clayton sleeve notes

1978

YOU TAKE MY HEART AWAY

On Record

Shirley Bassey

including
Silly love songs
C'est la vie
I need to be in love
If

You take my heart away

YOU TAKE MY HEART AWAY
PERFECT STRANGERS
SOMETIMES
THIS ONE'S FOR YOU
SILLY LOVE SONGS
STARGAZER
CAN'T HELP FALLING IN LOVE
I LET YOU LET ME DOWN AGAIN
IF
COME IN FROM THE RAIN
I NEED TO BE IN LOVE
C'EST LA VIE

1978

THE MAGIC IS YOU

hirley Bassey—The Magic Is You SHIRLEY BASSEY

YESTERDAYS

THIS IS MY LIFE
BETTER OFF ALONE
YOU NEVER DONE IT LIKE THAT
DON'T CRY FOR ME ARGENTINA
AS WE FALL IN LOVE ONCE MORE
NIGHT MOVES
ANYONE WHO HAD A HEART
THE MAGIC IS YOU
HOW INSENSITIVE
THE GREATEST LOVE OF ALL

MY MELANCHOLY BABY
I'M IN THE MOOD FOR LOVE
I'VE GOT YOU UNDER MY SKIN
TIME AFTER TIME
DON'T GET AROUND MUCH ANYMORE
THERE I'VE SAID IT AGAIN
YOU MADE ME LOVE YOU
OVER THE RAINBOW
TAKING A CHANCE ON LOVE
AS TIME GOES BY
I ONLY HAVE EYES FOR YOU
LOVE IS HERE TO STAY

1979

In Concert

ROYAL PERFORMANCE

PROGRAMME FOR THE
ROYAL PERFORMANCE
HELD AT THE WEMBLEY
CONFERENCE CENTRE
IN NOVEMBER 1979

WITH PRINCE CHARLES
AFTER THE ROYAL
PERFORMANCE

PROGRAMME
AND TICKET FOR THE
PUB ENTERTAINER
OF THE YEAR FINAL
AT THE ROYAL
ALBERT HALL

THEATRE PROGRAMME
SEPTEMBER 1979
BROADWAY
CONCERT

1979

124

1979 CONCERT
TOUR PROGRAMME
WITH TICKET

I've been told my voice has more in common with opera singers than with most singers of popular music. It's really to do with attack. I've always attacked a song. But in the beginning everybody said I was a 'belter', which used to upset me a little. 'Bassey belts the best.' Nobody could see that it was a little classical, that I was doing classical pop. But they didn't label me 'classical pop', because they couldn't think in those terms. They just called me either a pop singer or a belter.

Jessye Norman came to see me at Carnegie Hall, New York, about five, six years ago. She came backstage and said to me, 'How do you do it?' I looked in astonishment at her and replied, 'You are asking me how I do it? I mean, how do you do it? These great operas?' She explained, 'Ah but I'm on stage, you know, maybe three times during the whole performance. You do an hour and a half. One song after the other. I could never do that.' And I didn't walk out of the theatre. I floated out. Jessye Norman said that about me.

I fact, I do vocal exercises that opera singers do. About ten years ago I went to Helena Chanel, who taught me operatic vocal exercises, and that's how I keep the voice. Nowadays I train for about forty minutes before a show.

I was always losing my voice in the early years. After my daughter died, I lost it very often and began to think there was no way out of the problem. That's why my throat specialist eventually sent me to Helena. When I told Helena about it, she asked me, 'How do you do the E?' So I sang E. 'Wrong. That's how you're losing your voice,' she said. 'How?' I asked. 'E is the most difficult note to sing,' she explained, 'and the way you sing an E, you close your vocal cords.' 'Well, how can I do it?' So she told me to put my tongue behind my bottom teeth, and said, 'E is the vocal cord opening, feel it as I just sang it.' And since I've been doing the exercises, my voice has never let me down.

Helena is an excellent opera singer, with the patience of Job. She had to have, because when she was first teaching me, these vocal exercises were completely foreign to me. I'd never had a singing lesson. And as for vocal exercises, I'd never had those in my entire life. Nor had I ever been taught to read music. I still can't read a single note, so I have to go by my ear.

Luckily, the moment I hear something, I've got it. There might be a

couple of notes that I have to work on, though. So sometimes, in recording studios, it drives me insane because I've got the song but there are these notes that I might go flat or sharp on and my ear can only accept the proper note. So we have to work on these, and that means it takes a bit longer in the studio.

Helena also helped me discover new areas of the body that the voice comes from. She gave me an exercise one day and warned me it would sound strange. 'Because it sounds like a moo cow,' she explained. Oh gosh, I thought, what are we going to do now? Sure enough, it was 'Moooo'. I could feel the voice in my head, and the more we did this exercise the more head voice I had. Then Helena said, 'I've been listening, I've heard your records, but I've never heard you in a head voice before, and now I hear it.' I got very excited about that. We've struck gold here, I thought. And we had, because Helena had discovered I had an octave more than I thought I had. I'm beginning to use it more often now, especially on a record, though not so much on live performances, because in your hour and a half or two hours on stage you have to find a level where you're comfortable, and not overreach yourself. That's how you lose your voice.

Sometimes I find myself unconsciously doing that head voice, and it's a wonderful feeling. Helena taught me that it wasn't necessary to sing like that, to open your mouth wide to get a big note. You could open your mouth just a bit, and with the help of the exercises she taught me, bring out this big voice. To me this is extraordinary. I'm discovering all the time, from her exercises, new ways to place my voice. So that if, for instance, I have a cold, I can take it into the head voice, and nobody will know.

It's important to look after your voice, but there's no way you can survive the demands of live performance if you don't take care of your body too. I travel with a juicer and, as soon as I get up in the morning, my assistant makes me some fresh orange, apple or pineapple juice. Then I have a coffee and some wholewheat toast, jam and a mashed banana. After that I go to the gym for an hour. Then I stretch for half an hour, and afterwards I sit in a yoga position to do neck exercises and roll my head. At first I thought that all this was going to take my energy away, but it doesn't - it gives me incredible energy. And that I need: not only to throw my voice to the back of the auditorium, but also to be on stage as long as I am. I'm doing longer now than ever before. And with no pain at all at the end of it.

B A Shirley S E Y

131

I Am What I Am

U K **In Concert** A U T U M N T O U R

Apollo Victoria Theatre, London
WILTON ROAD, VICTORIA, LONDON

Apollo Leisure & MAM present

Shirley Bassey

IN CONCERT

STALLS Sunday
B 23 £17.50 Sept.
Evening

BARRY CLAYMAN CONCERTS PROUDLY PRESENTS

SHIRLEY BASSEY

IN CONCERT *plus* SUPPORT

Musical Director
MICHAEL ALEXANDER

FRIDAY, NOVEMBER 13th at 8pm
BLACKPOOL OPERA HOUSE
Box Office Tel: 0253 27786 Credit cards accepted
Ticket Prices: £26.50, £24.50, £20.50

1980
CONCERT TOUR
PROGRAMME,
TICKETS, PHOTOS
AND POSTER

1980

Shirley Bassey

ALL
BY
MYSELF

ALL BY MYSELF

THIS MASQUERADE

IF AND WHEN

HE'S OUT OF MY LIFE

NEW YORK STATE OF MIND

CAN YOU READ MY MIND

ONLY WHEN I LAUGH

SOLITAIRE

NEW YORK MEDLEY

WE DON'T CRY OUT LOUD

As one of the most popular singers in the world during the last two decades, Shirley Bassey is in a class of her own. Her distinctive style, which so successfully manages to express her varied experiences in so surprisingly rich lyrical terms, has won this outstanding artist a following all over the world.

By grafting the expressive richness of her black heritage onto her Welsh spontaneity, Shirley then assimilated - by mastering a rare technique - the traditional elegance of London town and the inventive inspiration of the Australian "new world" - two influences which were already apparent in her concerts during the early '60s.

Her success was instantaneous: the power in her voice and the sensitivity shown in her performances (harmonised in her sophisticated image), assured Shirley a vast following of "easy listening" fans in every corner of the globe and also enabled her within a short space of time to shoot to stardom and feel at home in any kind of repertory.

In Italy, for example, the fans (who'd already got to know her in '65 with the sensational hit *Goldfinger* - the title track from the James Bond film of the same name), acknowledged her stardom in '68 when she beautifully sang *La Vita* in Italian at the Sacremo Song Festival. From then on Shirley has remained a real favourite in Italy as a top artist, by keeping the hungry fans satisfied with the release of a long string of albums and through live and TV appearances which have always lived up to expectations.

Considered to be more of a concert than a "hit-parade" artist (there's nothing coincidental in the fact that she's one of the stars most in demand on the elegant Las Vegas stages), Shirley Bassey, whether she sings new songs especially written for her or "evergreens", always succeeds in conquering her audience: something that this album, which includes some of her best known hits, fully confirms.

Italian album sleeve notes

1982

In Concert

UK SEPTEMBER/OCTOBER TOUR

CONCERT PHOTOS,
OCTOBER 1982

1982

In Concert

BLAZER'S
FOURTH
ANNIVERSARY
CELEBRATIONS

February 1983

1985
BLAZER'S MENU
AND PHOTO

Shirley Bassey
To Sid
love Shirley Bassey

AT Blazer's

Bassey
at
BLAZER'S

May 1984

1983
BLAZER'S MENU
AND PHOTO

1984
BLAZER'S MENU
AND PHOTO

1983-5

On Record

I AM WHAT I AM   LA MUJER

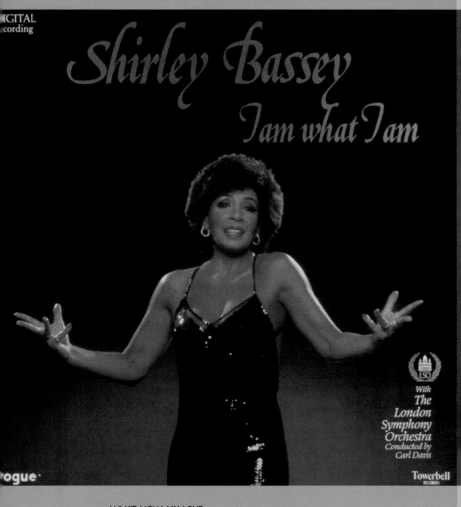

WHAT NOW MY LOVE

SOMETHING

AS LONG AS HE NEEDS ME

KISS ME HONEY HONEY

AS I LOVE YOU

BIG SPENDER

SEND IN THE CLOWNS

I AM WHAT I AM

GOLDFINGER

I (WHO HAVE NOTHING)

NATALIE

AND I LOVE YOU SO

NEVER NEVER NEVER

FOR ALL WE KNOW

THIS IS MY LIFE

LA PASION QUE NOS DEVORA

SIN TI (WITHOUT YOU)

VOLVERAS

NO ME HABLES MAS DE AMOR

NADIE MAS TE QUISO (COMO YO) (I COULD NEVER MISS YOU MORE THAN I DO)

ASI SOLA YO (OUT HERE ON MY OWN)

NO FINGIRE

HOY NO TENGO NADA (I WHO HAVE NOTHING)

VALLAS (RIVALS)

SI YO TE QUIERO MAS

1984/9

Shirley Bassey

I have to tell you that this album was not easy for me to make for the simple reason that I do not speak Spanish. No, really I do not, but I did invest in twenty hours of Spanish lessons which proved invaluable because I was able to sing the actual Spanish words and not use phonetics. I, also have to tell you that I am very proud of my first effort! No matter what language you speak the language of love is universal. I dedicate this album with all my love to you.

1984
CONCERT
PROGRAMME
COVER

In Concert

ST DAVID'S HALL, CARDIFF

1985
ST DAVID'S HALL
GALA CHARITY
CONCERT POSTER

1985
ST DAVID'S HALL
CONCERT
PROGRAMME

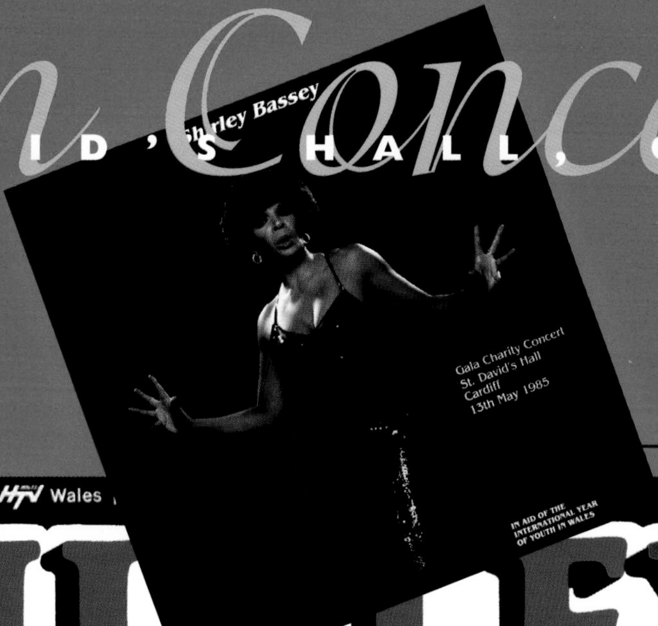

Shirley Bassey
Gala Charity Concert
St. David's Hall
Cardiff
13th May 1985
IN AID OF THE INTERNATIONAL YEAR OF YOUTH IN WALES

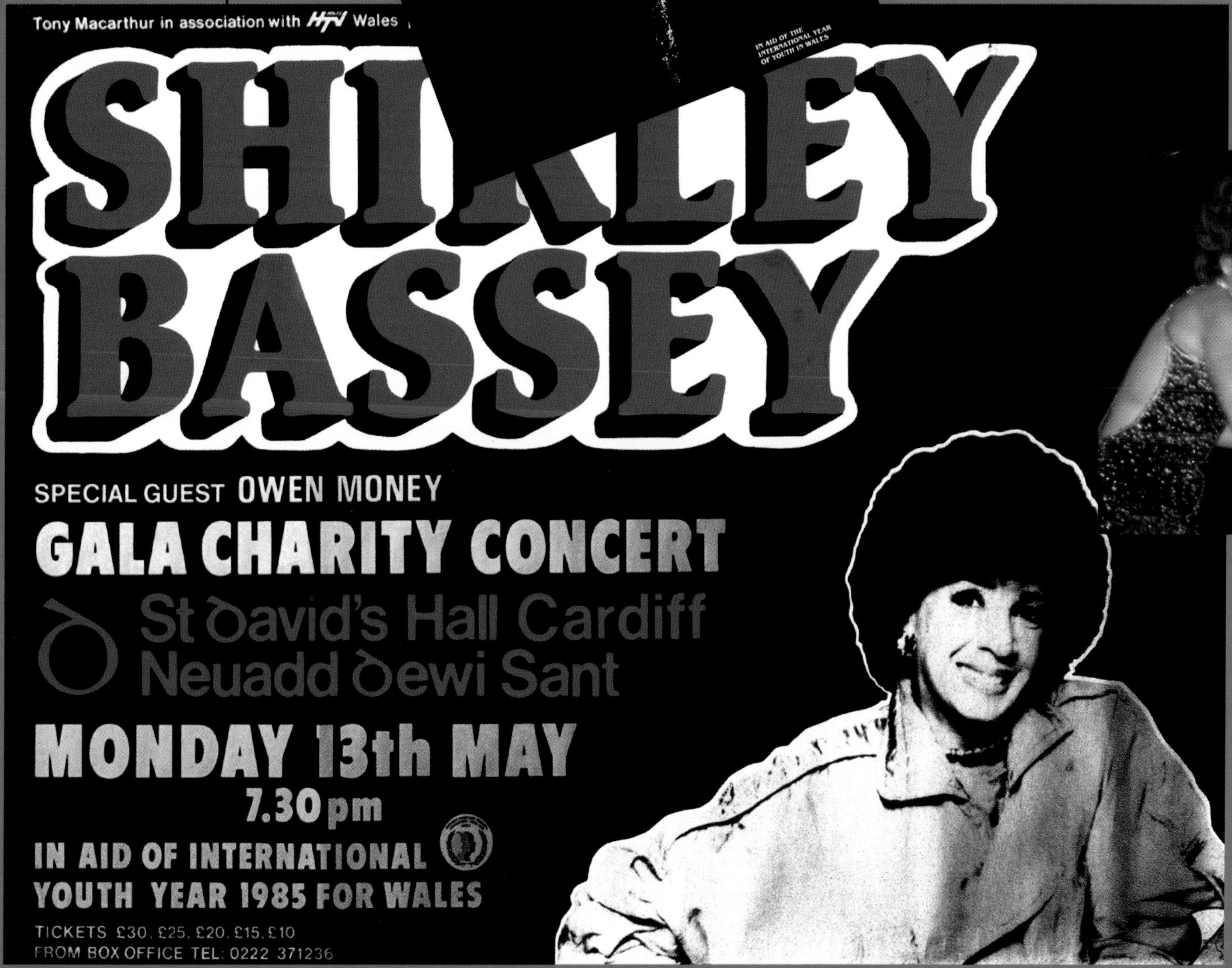

Tony Macarthur in association with HTV Wales
SHIRLEY BASSEY
SPECIAL GUEST OWEN MONEY
GALA CHARITY CONCERT
St David's Hall Cardiff
Neuadd Dewi Sant
MONDAY 13th MAY
7.30pm
IN AID OF INTERNATIONAL YOUTH YEAR 1985 FOR WALES
TICKETS £30. £25. £20. £15. £10
FROM BOX OFFICE TEL: 0222 371236

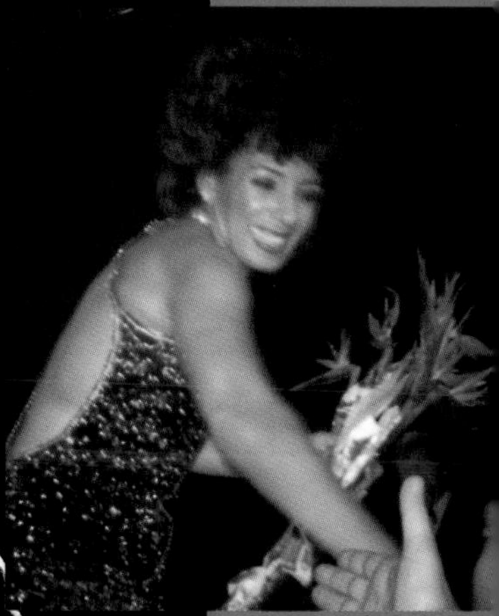

1985

Hi everyone
thanks for coming It's great to be back We're all going to have
a great time tonight. Love + Best wishes   Shirley Bassey

In Concert

Australia

Austria

Canada

England

France

Germany

Holland

Hong Kong

Ireland

Japan

Poland

Scotland

Sri Lanka

Turkey

United Arab Emirates

USA

Wales

SHIRLEY BASSEY

1986
WORLD TOUR
PROGRAMME

USA
24 JUNE
SUMMER OF STARS
PROGRAMME

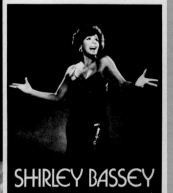

USA
9 JULY
MARQUIS
THEATRE
PROGRAMME

1986

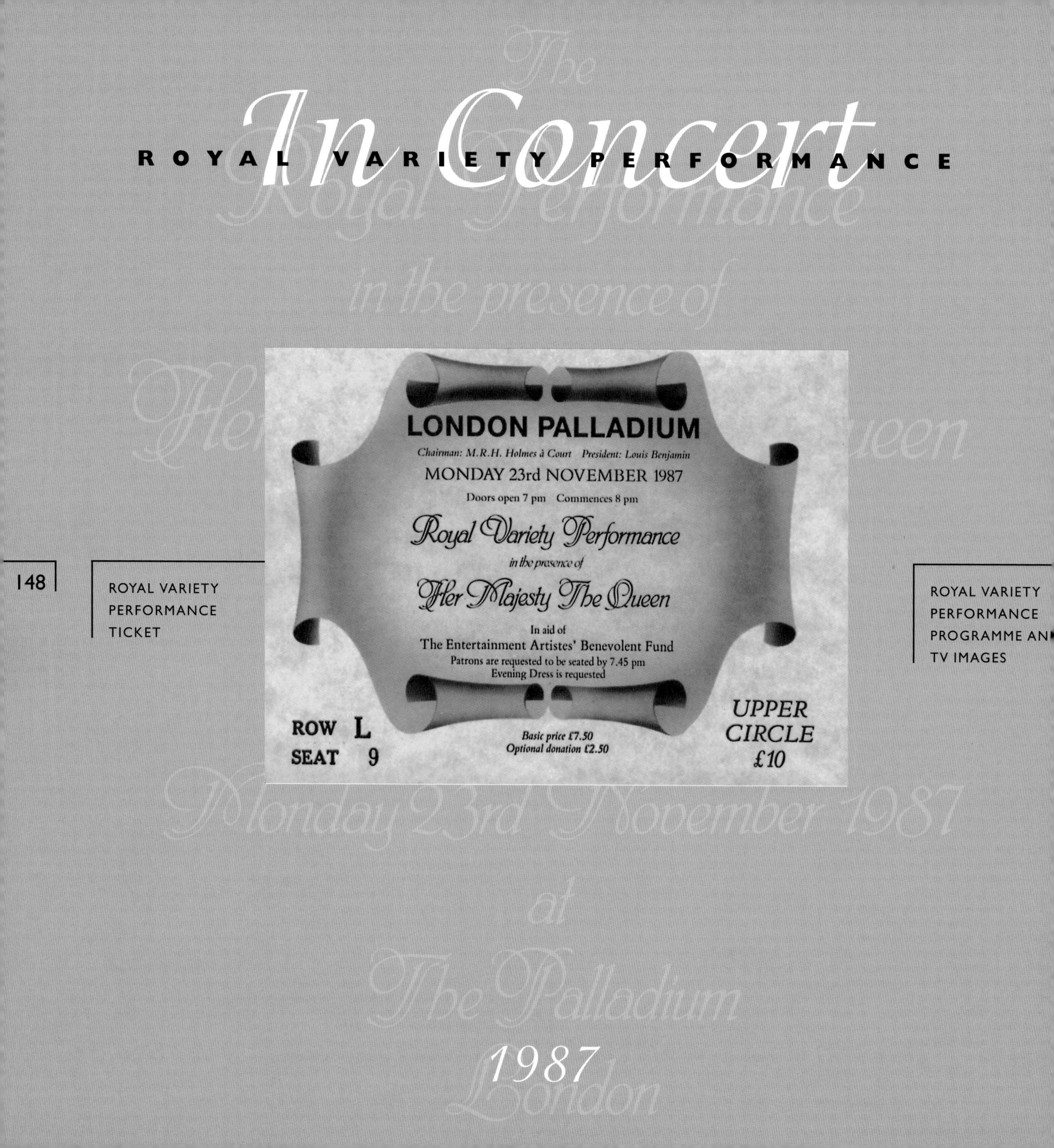

In Concert

ROYAL VARIETY
PERFORMANCE
TICKET

LONDON PALLADIUM

Chairman: M.R.H. Holmes à Court   President: Louis Benjamin

MONDAY 23rd NOVEMBER 1987

Doors open 7 pm   Commences 8 pm

Royal Variety Performance

in the presence of

Her Majesty The Queen

In aid of
The Entertainment Artistes' Benevolent Fund

Patrons are requested to be seated by 7.45 pm
Evening Dress is requested

ROW **L**
SEAT **9**

Basic price £7.50
Optional donation £2.50

**UPPER
CIRCLE
£10**

ROYAL VARIETY
PERFORMANCE
PROGRAMME AN
TV IMAGES

The Royal Performance in the presence of Her Majesty The Queen
Monday 23rd November 1987 at The Palladium 1987 London

The
Royal Performance
in the presence of
Her Majesty The Queen

at 8pm
on the evening of
Monday 23rd November 1987
at
The Palladium
London

SHIRLEY
BASSEY
ONVERGE FEEL LIKE
HITS

ecord
1980s

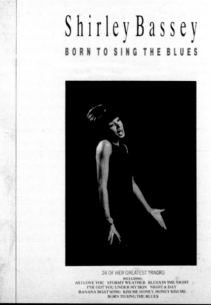

Shirley Bassey
BORN TO SING THE BLUES

24 OF HER GREATEST TRACKS
INCLUDING:
AS I LOVE YOU STORMY WEATHER BLUES IN THE NIGHT
I'VE GOT YOU UNDER MY SKIN NIGHT & DAY
BANANA BOAT SONG KISS ME HONEY, HONEY KISS ME
BORN TO SING THE BLUES

EDICION ESPECIAL
COLECCIONISTAS

DISCOGRAFIA
COMPLETA

LO MEJOR DE SHIRLEY BASSE

20
FABULOUS
TRACKS
20 TEMAS FABULOSOS

SHIRLEY BASSEY

super hits

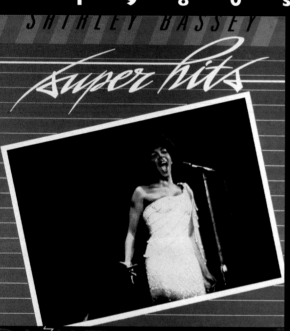

*Shirley
Bassey
Tonight*

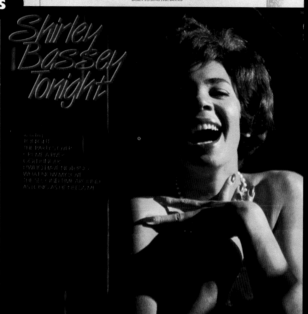

SHIRLEY BASSEY'S GREATEST HI
GOLDFINGER / SOMETHING / FEELINGS / DIAMONDS ARE FOREVER / WHAT I DID FOR LOVE / I'LL BE YOUR AL
FOR ALL WE KNOW / YESTERDAY, WHEN I WAS YOUNG / THE GREAT PERFORMANCE OF MY LIFE / L CAP

SHIRLEY
BASSEY

As I Love You

luding
AS I LOVE YOU
KISS HONEY KISS ME
BANANA BOAT SONG
NIGHT AND DAY
STORMY WEATHER

Shirley Bassey

AND I LOVE YOU SO
KILLING ME SOFTLY WITH HIS SONG
AND WE WERE LOVERS
YOU ARE THE SUNSHINE OF MY LIFE
YESTERDAY I HEARD THE RAIN
WHERE DO I BEGIN (LOVE STORY)
SPINNING WHEEL
YOU'RE GONNA HEAR FROM ME
LET ME SING AND I AM HAPPY
THE SOUND OF MUSIC
STRANGERS IN THE NIGHT
I'VE NEVER BEEN A WOMAN BEFORE
THE WAY A WOMAN LOVES
BABY I'M A WANT YOU
WITHOUT YOU
LIGHT MY FIRE

Shirley

UK TOUR *In Concert* APRIL-MAY

ST DAVID'S HALL,
CARDIFF,
CONCERT PHOTOS

152

1988

AT THE ROYAL
ALBERT HALL

Shirley

BASSEY

with Special Guest
TED ROGERS

B.I.C., BOURNEMOUTH
SUNDAY 1st & TUESDAY 3rd MAY at 7.30 p.m.

BOURNEMOUTH
CONCERT
POSTER

GUEST
BACKSTAGE
PASS

Shirley

K TOUR 1988

GUEST

FTER SHOW
ONLY

ROYA   RT HALL
GENER   MERON McNICOL
THE FACE OF   A COLOURED BACKGROUND
WEDNES   MAY 1988.
AT 1930   PEN AT 1845
DUDLEY   PRESENTS
S   LEY BASSEY
IN CONCERT
WITH GUEST ARTIST.
ADMIT TO:
ARENA 'A'
ENTER BY DOOR 2
PRICE (INC. VAT)   ROW   SEAT
3 0341 N   £25.00   3   2
BACK OF THIS DOCUMENT CONTAINS AN ARTIFICIAL WATERMARK
O BE RETAINED   See Reverse

Shirley

153

CONCERT TOUR
PROGRAMME

ROYAL ALBERT
HALL TICKET
AND PHOTOS

BOURNEMOUTH

MANCHESTER

CARDIFF

In Concert

CARDIFF

155

1989

My Life in Song

At rehearsal I can be nervous or I can be very calm. There's a saying in show business that if you have a good rehearsal you can have a bad show. It's a superstition, but it never leaves you, especially when you've come from the old school of show business that I came from, Variety. Those old superstitions linger on. For instance, never let anybody whistle in the dressing room and if they do you must send them out and they must turn round three times and knock on the door. Invariably I don't tell them to come in again, so they're standing there, outside. When it's been a bad rehearsal I console myself with the fact that it's going to be a great show. But when it's a good rehearsal I still get nervous.

Those things stay with you. Somebody wishing you good luck, for example. That's the kiss of death. Many years ago, when Sunday Night at the London Palladium was live, I was about to take my position backstage before the curtains opened, when somebody said, 'Good luck, Shirley.' The curtain opened, I walked out and started the song, and then forgot the words. It was only for a split second, but even so, that's every singer's nightmare.
I just shut myself off the moment I leave the stage after rehearsal. It's a quiet time for me, and only the people who are close to me are allowed anywhere near. I don't want to be rattled, or have to raise my voice, becauseI feel that if I do I might lose it.

I just concentrate on my make-up. I don't do any exercises. It's basically a time for relaxing, and I just go into myself. And as I'm making up, I'm thinking of the songs that I'm going to sing. Of course, if one of the songs went badly in rehearsal, then that's on my mind and I keep going over that song to make sure that I stay focused on it, to avoid making the same mistake. Really, the whole preparation time is a time for focusing, for concentrating on what I'm about to do when I walk out onto that stage.

I have nothing alcoholic to drink. I might have a coffee, and I'll sip a lot of cold water, especially when I'm nervous, because it helps, just sipping. I'll occasionally break out into my vocals, just to make sure my voice is still there.
Beforehand, I'm sometimes very nervous, and if I get very jumpy and feel that it's going to upset my performance, I take myself into a corner and just shout. I make sure that I shout in the key that I'm about to sing in, so that it won't upset the vocal cords. And it does help. I remember a time when I was so nervous at the Pigalle in London, and it never left me throughout the performance; it was

devastating. Afterwards I said, 'I never want to go through that again. If I ever do I'll stop singing.' But then I asked myself: Why were you so nervous? Why couldn't you control the nerves after the first, second, third number? When I analysed it, I found that I'd lost my focus, that I was thinking about something that was happening at home. So I had to teach myself never to take domestic matters like that on stage with me.

On the other hand, my songs do represent chunks of my life, of my own personal history. But the difference is that they're past history - I can't take the present on stage. I sing certain songs in a particular way because I've experienced what I'm singing about. If I were to take on stage with me something that was bothering me at present, I wouldn't be able to concentrate, to focus. And that's what happened that night.

When people ask me about the sort of things that might unsettle me on stage, I say that if it goes wrong it's in me, not the audience. Somebody distracting me, for instance, that doesn't worry me, because I'm very good if people in the audience call out. In fact, back in the old days in Variety they used to do that and I answered back and loved it.

No, it's always within me. It's something I've taken something on stage: a thought, a problem. So I mustn't take any baggage on with me, except maybe from the past, to put into those songs. The songs are what I have to focus on and nothing but the present can be allowed to shape them. That may sound tough, but that's how it is for me. To come as far as I have is a matter of having tremendous discipline, which I never had at one time. I'd party, and go to nightclubs until two or three in the morning. Then I'd go and do shows. But I realized as I got older that I couldn't do those things and two shows a night. Fortunately, on stage I had the presence of mind to make my nervousness into a movement so that people couldn't see that I was jumpy.

In a sense, being on stage is a way of dealing with pain, with confusion and vulnerability. There are times, when I'm not performing, when I wake up feeling terribly vulnerable for some unknown reason. Maybe I've had a dream or I've been worrying about something before going to bed. The best thing to bring me back on track is to go to the gym and work out. Then I'm focused once again, and I can handle it.

B A *Shirley* S E Y

The Show Must Go On

SHIRLEY BASSEY

WITH SPECIAL GUEST WAYNE DOBSON

A ROYAL GALA EVENING

IN AID OF

THE PRINCE'S TRUST

IN THE PRESENCE OF

THEIR ROYAL HIGHNESSES

THE PRINCE AND PRINCESS OF WALES

AT

THE LONDON PALLADIUM
WEDNESDAY, 5TH DECEMBER, 1990

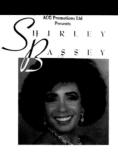

ACG Promotions Ltd
Presents

SHIRLEY BASSEY

Saturday 12th June
&
Sunday 13th June
8.00 pm
at Fort Regent, Jersey
Also featuring Adrian Walsh and full Supporting Band
Tickets available from Fort Regent Box Office
Telephone 0534 500227

USA
FORT REGENT
POSTERS

A ROYAL GALA EVENING

In Concert

THE
PRINCE'S TRUST
CONCERT
LONDON

MANCHESTER
1990

NEC
BIRMINGHAM

1990

In Concert

U K T O U R 1 9 9 1

1991

ON STAGE AT LONDON'S
ROYAL ALBERT HALL

THE SECOND TIME
I HAVE BEEN CAUGHT
FOR *THIS IS YOUR LIFE* —
THIS TIME BY HOST
MICHAEL ASPEL

THIS IS YOUR LIFE - AGAIN!

In Concert

1992

SONGS OF ANDREW LLOYD WEBBER

MEMORY

STARLIGHT EXPRESS

ALL I ASK OF YOU

I DON'T KNOW HOW TO LOVE HIM

MACAVITY

CHANSON D'ENFANCE

WITH ONE LOOK

TELL ME ON A SUNDAY

THE LAST MAN IN MY LIFE

DON'T CRY FOR ME ARGENTINA

WISHING YOU WERE SOMEONE HERE AGAIN

AS IF WE NEVER SAID GOODBYE

MEMORY (REPRISE)

167

This new exciting album opens a new chapter in the illustrious career of this great lady. Over the past twenty years the theatres in the capital cities of the world have become increasingly dominated by the musicals of Sir Andrew Lloyd Webber. It was perhaps inevitable that eventually these two great names would be linked in a unique recording of the biggest and most successful Lloyd Webber songs.

The music spans the complete career of the great composer. *I Don't Know To Love Him* from his early musical *Jesus Christ Superstar*, written in collaboration with Tim Rice, through to *Don't Cry For Me Argentina* and *Evita* and on to his more recent works from *Phantom* and *Aspects* namely *Wishing You Were Somehow Here Again*, *All I Ask Of You* and *Chanson D'Enfance*. The recording also features the two big numbers from his most recent success *Sunset Boulevard*, *As If We Never Said Goodbye* and of course *With One Look*.

Every song is sung with that special magic that comes from the performer who makes every word count and who always sings straight from the heart. As someone said in the studio during the actual recording "It's as if they had all been written especially for Shirley". The songs cover such wide range of styles and interpretations from the Big Band swing numbers *Starlight Express* and *Macavity* to the tender love songs from *Song & Dance*, *The Last Man In My Life* and *Tell Me On A Sunday*.

A special recording the music of the greatest composer of our age sung by someone who can only be described as the one and only SHIRLEY BASSEY.

Gordon Lorenz sleeve notes

1993

CBE

SHIRLEY BASSEY CBE

AT BUCKINGHAM
PALACE AFTER
RECEIVING MY CBE
FROM HER MAJESTY
THE QUEEN

WITH MY
DAUGHTER SHARON
AND MY CLOSE
FRIENDS BEAUDOIN
AND YVES MILLS

1993

In Concert

BRISTOL, CARDIFF & UTRECHT

A WARM
WELCOME IN
BRISTOL

1993

GALA CONCERT

ZATERDAG 6 NOVEMBER 1993
DE PRINS VAN ORANJEHAL
KONINKLIJKE JAARBEURS, UTRECHT, AANVANG 20.00 UUR

ny Charles · Liza Minnelli · Shirley Bassey

VAK	A	RIJ	3	STOEL	23

Shirley Bassey
in concert

BRISTOL CITY COUNCIL in ASSOCIATION
with SHINE ENTERTAINMENT PRESENT

Miss Shirley Bassey

SEAT	PRICE
1	22.00

CANONS MARSH
AMPHITHEATRE,
BRISTOL CITY DOCKS

CIA

IMG Artists
Proudly Present

THE GALA OPENING CONCERT OF
CARDIFF INTERNATIONAL ARENA

SHIRLEY BASSEY
COMES HOME!

FRIDAY 10th SEPTEMBER 1993
DOORS 7.00pm   SHOWTIME 8.00pm
£32.50 (Subject to Booking Fee)

ARENA SEATING
BLOCK : 2
ROW: A   SEAT: 26   00506

TEN THOUSAND AND ONE VOICES

Côr y Byd · The World Choir
Sunday, September 19, 8.15
888

JUNE 24 -25

TONIGHT

SHIRLEY
BASSEY

12-PAGE SPECIAL

EVENING POST

KEEP THE MUSIC PLAYING   **SINGS THE MOVIES**

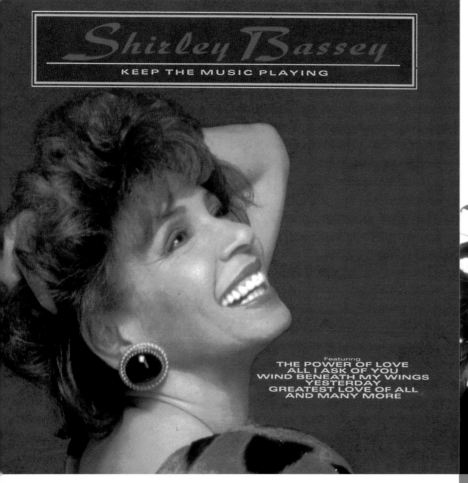

HOW DO YOU KEEP THE MUSIC PLAYING

HE WAS BEAUTIFUL

THE POWER OF LOVE

STILL

ALL I ASK OF YOU

I WANT TO KNOW WHAT LOVE IS

WIND BENEATH MY WINGS

YESTERDAY

THAT'S WHAT FRIENDS ARE FOR

SORRY SEEMS TO BE THE HARDEST WORD

GREATEST LOVE OF ALL

DIO COME TI-AMO (OH GOD HOW MUCH I LOVE YOU)

GOLDFINGER

CRAZY

ARTHUR'S THEME (BEST THAT YOU CAN DO)

LOVE ON THE ROCKS

ELEANOR RIGBY

LET'S STAY TOGETHER

THE ROSE

WE DON'T NEED ANOTHER HERO

DO YOU KNOW WHERE YOU'RE GOING TO

IT MUST HAVE BEEN LOVE

TRY A LITTLE TENDERNESS

HOPELESSLY DEVOTED TO YOU

MAKIN' WHOOPEE

WHO WANTS TO LIVE FOREVER

1991/95

THE SHOW MUST GO ON   THE BIRTHDAY CONCERT

SHIRLEY BASSEY
The Show Must Go On

INCLUDING

HELLO

[CA]N I TOUCH YOU THERE

[SL]AVE TO THE RHYTHM

BABY COME TO ME

WHEN I NEED YOU

YOU'LL SEE

AND MANY MORE

Shirley
BASSEY
The Birthday Concert

SLAVE TO THE RHYTHM
YOU'LL SEE
EVERY BREATH YOU TAKE
CAN I TOUCH YOU THERE
I'LL STAND BY YOU
WHEN I NEED YOU
ALL WOMAN
HE KILLS EVERYTHING
WHERE IS THE LOVE
WE'VE GOT TONIGHT
ONE DAY I'LL FLY AGAIN
HELLO
BABY COME TO ME
THE SHOW MUST GO ON

1996/7

S'WONDERFUL
DIAMONDS ARE FOREVER
NOBODY DOES IT LIKE ME
NEVER, NEVER, NEVER
KISS ME, HONEY, HONEY
BIG SPENDER
LADY IS A TRAMP
NEW YORK, NEW YORK
WHAT NOW MY LOVE
SOMETHING
HEY JUDE
I WANNA KNOW WHAT LOVE IS
LA PASSIONE
I WHO HAVE NOTHING
YESTERDAY, WHEN I WAS YOUNG
THIS IS MY LIFE
I WISH YOU LOVE
I AM WHAT I AM

SOUVENIR OF
MY SWITCHING ON
BLACKPOOL LIGHTS

BLACKPOOL
40TH ANNIVERSARY
TOUR POSTER

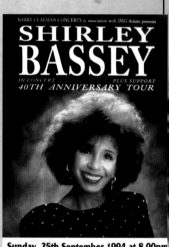

MELBOURNE HILTON
DINNER AND SHOW
MENU AND PROGRAMME

In Concert

VARIETY CLUB
GREAT BRITAIN

THE GREATEST
CHILDREN'S CHARITY
IN THE WORLD

Tribute Luncheon to

VARIETY CLUB TRIBUTE LUNCHEON MENU

The Shirley Bassey 40th Anniversary Concert Tour: The Royal Festival Hall

Bassey's back on song and a star is reborn

THE last time I saw Shirley Bassey perform she had become so much a grotesque parody of her own stage persona that I had seen drag comics do impressions of her which were less funny by far.

And, if my memory serves me right for it is many years and one CBE ago now, I said so in less than gentlemanly fashion.

Well, as my favourite TV chat show host, the sensitively-challenged Alan Partridge is so fond of saying: here is a plate with words on it, get your knife and fork ready to eat them, Mr Clever Clogs Critic.

For time and bitter experience have tempered Bassey's wayward mannerisms and harnessed that unpredictable diction.

Now, on this 40th anniversary tour of her show-business debut, she is to

JACK TINKER
AT LAST NIGHT'S FIRST NIGHT

be classed with the finest songstresses in this or any other land.

A unique and compelling performance to be put alongside those other international legends of song and glamour, the Josephine Bakers and the Dietrichs. Moreover, she can work on an audience to the point of hysteria reminiscent of a Garland.

In short, the sort of phenomenon in increasingly sparse supply.

especially on these shores.

What changed the self-indulgence which once threatened to overwhelm her undoubted talent was the shock of losing her voice on stage shortly after the death of her daughter.

A leading voice coach came to the rescue, forbidding all those facial distortions and the vocal strangulations.

The result today is a voice of almost operatic

power and purity blessed with a deeper, richer timbre than before. And with it a rediscovered respect for all the songs she sings.

There is something approaching girlish awe in her version of the Beatles' Something. And she bestows on Andrew Lloyd Webber's Sunset Boulevard hits such unimpeachable authority that you wonder why no one thought to offer her the part in the first place.

Only Dame Maggie Smith is possessed of more expressive hands than she, but Dame Maggie is hardly likely to belt, bump or grind her way through Big Spender — though, come to think of it, neither is Miss Bassey about to bring the house down with her Desdemona.

However, the wide theatrical gestures are now entirely appropriate to the emotions of her numbers. And shimmering her way through 15 routines in a transparent sheath of white-tasselled silver, she proves, to paraphrase one of her own songs, that nobody does it like Bassey.

She is a born-again star to be taken very seriously indeed.

Shirley Bassey CBE

THE SAVOY
LONDON

Friday 25th November 1994

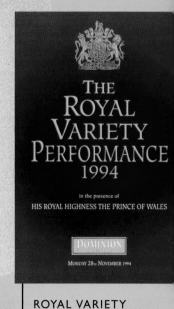

ROYAL VARIETY PERFORMANCE PROGRAMME

1994

AN AUDIENCE WITH SHIRLEY BASSEY

TV IMAGES FROM
*AN AUDIENCE WITH
SHIRLEY BASSEY*

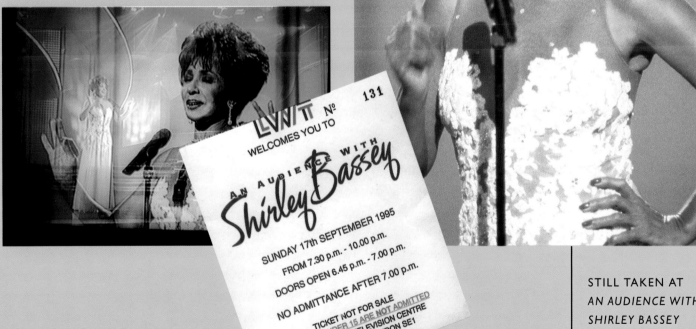

LWT № 131
WELCOMES YOU TO

AN AUDIENCE WITH
Shirley Bassey

SUNDAY 17th SEPTEMBER 1995
FROM 7.30 p.m. - 10.00 p.m.
DOORS OPEN 6.45 p.m. - 7.00 p.m.
NO ADMITTANCE AFTER 7.00 p.m.
TICKET NOT FOR SALE
CHILDREN UNDER 15 ARE NOT ADMITTED
AT THE LONDON TELEVISION CENTRE
UPPER GROUND LONDON SE1
ADMIT ONE

STILL TAKEN AT
*AN AUDIENCE WITH
SHIRLEY BASSEY*

1996

HANDBILL AND
PROGRAMME FOR
OSLO CONCERT

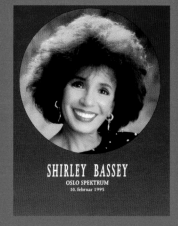

CARDIFF CASTLE
CONCERT PHOTO
AND TICKET

HOARDING OUTSIDE
CARDIFF CASTLE

MOBILE POSTER
SEEN THROUGHOUT
CARDIFF

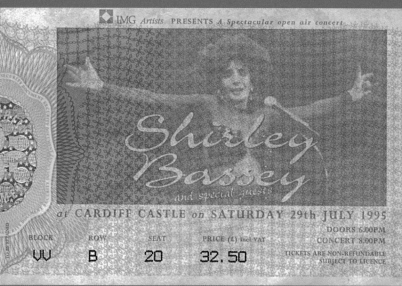

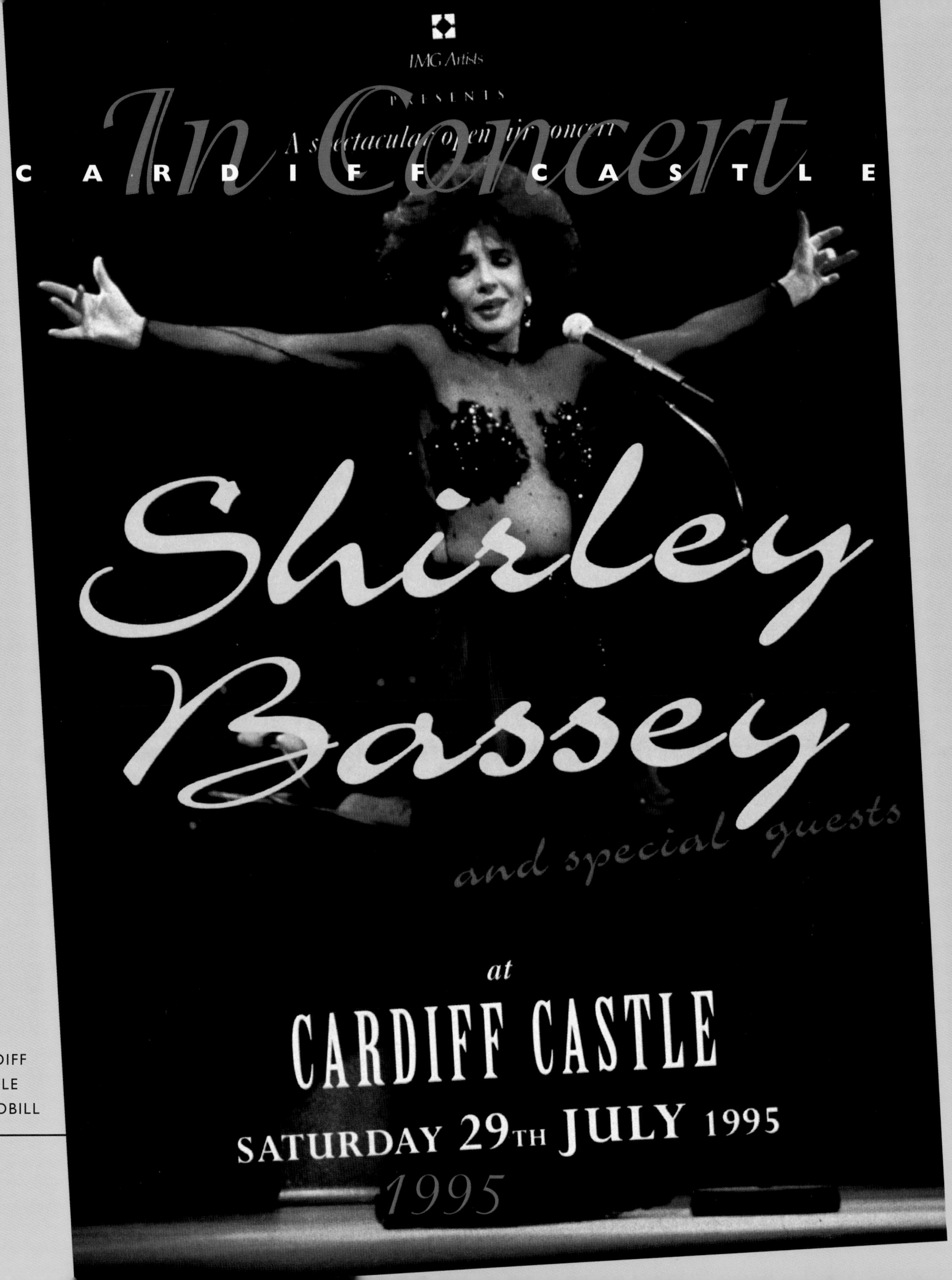

IMG Artists

PRESENTS

A spectacular open air concert

CARDIFF CASTLE

In Concert

Shirley Bassey

and special guests

at

CARDIFF CASTLE

SATURDAY 29TH JULY 1995

1995

CARDIFF
CASTLE
HANDBILL

1996
CONCERT TOUR
POSTER

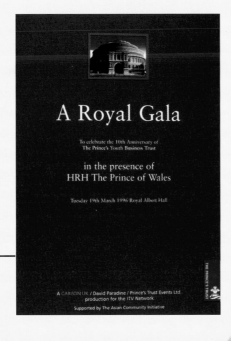

BARRY CLAYMAN CONCERTS in association with IMG ARTISTS presents

SHIRLEY BASSEY
IN CONCERT   PLUS SUPPORT

SOLD OUT

BRIGHTON CENTRE 28th APRIL
NOTTINGHAM ROYAL CONCERT HALL
30th APRIL, 7th & 8th MAY
LIVERPOOL EMPIRE 1st MAY
BLACKPOOL OPERA HOUSE 3rd-4th MAY
SHEFFIELD ARENA 5th MAY
BIRMINGHAM NEC 10th MAY

NEWCASTLE ARENA 11th MAY
GLASGOW GICH 13th, 14th, 15th MAY
MANCHESTER NYNEX ARENA 18th MAY
CARDIFF CIA 19th-20th MAY
PLYMOUTH PAVILIONS 22nd MAY
BRISTOL HIPPODROME 23rd MAY
BOURNEMOUTH BIC 25th-26th MAY

1996
CONCERT TOUR
PROGRAMME

Shirley

ROYAL
FESTIVAL HALL,
LONDON

181

ROYAL GALA
CONCERT
PROGRAMME

A Royal Gala

To celebrate the 10th Anniversary of
The Prince's Youth Business Trust

in the presence of
HRH The Prince of Wales

Tuesday 19th March 1996 Royal Albert Hall

A CARLTON UK / David Paradine / Prince's Trust Events Ltd.
production for the ITV Network

Supported by The Asian Community Initiative

og NGM presenterer i samarbeid med VG
IMG Artists

One of the world's greatest entertainers

Shirley Bassey
on tour '96
med eget band

"Shirley Bassey reminds
us what show business
is all about"
The Guardian 5.10.94

6. mars - Olavshallen
i Trondheim
8. mars - Hjertnessalen
i Sandefjord.
10. mars - Stavanger
Konserthus

Kuallgod diva!

*Glamour og
kjærlighet!*

"To me, show business is
about glamour"
Shirley Bassey

Hovedsponsor: Statnett

NORWEGIAN
CONCERT
HANDBILL

1996

La Passione

WITH THE
PROPELLERHEADS,
WHO WROTE
HISTORY REPEATING

WITH CHRIS REA,
WHO WROTE THE
LA PASSIONE
SCREENPLAY

1996

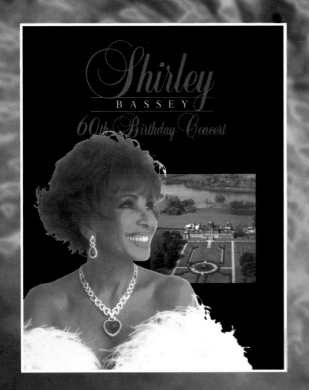

BIRTHDAY CONCERT
ALTHORP PARK

In Concert

I was delighted to be celebrating my 60th birthday on stage with two outdoor shows, at Castle Howard on 19 July and Althorp Park on 26 July. I was thrilled to be marking this occasion with so many of my fans and couldn't have imagined a more perfect backdrop for my birthday party.

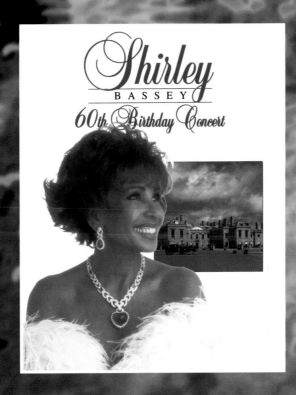

BIRTHDAY CONCERT
CASTLE HOWARD

1997

CHOOSING DRESSES

Before a show, I always have a definite idea of the dress or dresses that I'll wear, and I will want, say, that top and that bottom and that middle. And I'll want it in one dress, so I'll call up Douglas Darnell or Sarah Perceval and tell them my idea. They'll send me three or even six drawings of what they think I want, and one of them will be near what I'm looking for. Sometimes it's awfully difficult. One night I might feel I like the tasselled gowns that Doug made, the white tassel and black tassel. But how do I follow these two dresses? And then Sarah comes up with the white chiffon and the black chiffon, and I've worn those, practically worn them out. Again, how do I follow those? One of the two is going to have to come out.

It's got to look spectacular on stage, because that's what it's all about. I can't just wear a simple dress. I have simple dresses in my wardrobe that I wear to dinner parties. I can't wear a stage gown to a dinner party, because I can't sit in it. So I want something glamorous that I can't wear out. Something outrageous even. I'm looking for something different all the time.

Some of the dresses feel incredibly heavy, especially when you've been used to wearing one that's light. I might suddenly decide to wear one of the heavy ones, but then I have to be very clever because if I do a turn it's so heavy I might go into a spin like a top and not stop!

I still have my first gown from when I was eighteen years old. Doug Darnell made that one for me. It was sexy, and it was heavy because it was all diamanté.

Of course, the whole stage thing is showing off. The fact that I walk on in front of thousands of people and sing, that's showing off to begin with, so why not do it with a spectacular gown? Not go on in jeans - anybody can do that. I don't wear clothes like that offstage either. I'm very conservative in my choice of clothes offstage.

One side of me is the glamorous, romantic side. The other is still that little girl that left home at sixteen. I didn't go through my teenage years like any other teenager, with lots of boys coming round to pick you up and take you to the local dance. I missed all that. The girl offstage, Shirley Bassey offstage, sort of dreams about that, I suppose. I've always been a dreamer, and that's what helps me to do what I do on stage.

SINGLES

Year	Cat. No.	Title
78RPM		
1956	Philips PB 558	BURN MY CANDLE/STORMY WEATHER
1956	Philips PB 598	THE WAYWARD WIND/BORN TO SING THE BLUES
1956	Philips PB 651	AFTER THE LIGHTS GO DOWN/IF YOU DON'T LOVE ME
1957	Philips PB 668	THE BANANA BOAT SONG/TRA LA LA
1957	Philips PB 673	IF I HAD A NEEDLE AND THREAD/TONIGHT MY HEART SHE IS CRYING
1957	Phillps PB 723	FIRE DOWN BELOW/YOU, YOU ROMEO
1957	Philips PB 757	PUH-LEEZE! MISTER BROWN/TAKE MY LOVE, TAKE MY LOVE
1958	Philips PB 845	AS I LOVE YOU/HANDS ACROSS THE SEA
1958	Philips PB 860	KISS ME, HONEY HONEY, KISS ME/THERE'S NEVER BEEN A NIGHT
1959	Columbla DB 4344	IF YOU LOVE ME/COUNT ON ME
45RPM		
1957	Philips JK 1006	THE BANANA BOAT SONG/TRA LA LA
1957	Philips JK 1018	IF I HAD A NEEDLE AND THREAD/TONIGHT MY HEART SHE IS CRYING
1957	Philips JK 1034	PUH-LEEZE! MISTER BROWN/TAKE MY LOVE, TAKE MY LOVE
1958	Philips PB 845	AS I LOVE YOU/HANDS ACROSS THE SEA
1958	Philips PB 860	KISS ME, HONEY HONEY, KISS ME/THERE'S NEVER BEEN A NIGHT
1959	Philips PB 917	LOVE FOR SALE/CRAZY RHYTHM
1959	Phillps PB 919	MY FUNNY VALENTINE/HOW ABOUT YOU?
1959	Philips PB 975	NIGHT AND DAY/THE GYPSY IN MY SOUL
1959	Columbia DB 4344	IF YOU LOVE ME/COUNT ON ME
1960	Columbia DB 4421	WITH THESE HANDS/THE PARTY'S OVER
1960	Phillps BF 1091	THE BIRTH OF THE BLUES/THE CARELESS LOVE BLUES
1960	Columbia DB 4490	AS LONG AS HE NEEDS ME/SO IN LOVE
1961	Columbia DB 4643	YOU'LL NEVER KNOW/HOLD ME TIGHT
1961	Columbia DB 4685	REACH FOR THE STARS/CLIMB EV'RY MOUNTAIN
1961	Columbia DB 4737	I'LL GET BY/WHO ARE WE?
1962	Columbia DB 4777	TONIGHT/LET'S START ALL OVER AGAIN
1962	Columbia DB 4816	AVE MARIA/YOU'LL NEVER WALK ALONE
1962	Columbia DB 4836	FAR AWAY/MY FAITH
1962	Columbia DB 4882	WHAT NOW MY LOVE?/ABOVE ALL THINGS
1963	Columbia DB 4974	WHAT KIND OF FOOL AM I?/TILL
1963	Columbia DB 7113	I (WHO HAVE NOTHING)/HOW CAN YOU TELL?
1963	Philips 326565 BF	PUH-LEEZE! MISTER BROWN/THE WAYWARD WIND
1964	Columbia DB 7185	MY SPECIAL DREAM/YOU
1964	Columbia DB 7248	GONE/YOUR LOVE
1964	Columbia DB 7337	WHO CAN I TURN TO?/TO BE LOVED BY A MAN
1964	Columbia DB 7360	GOLDFINGER/STRANGE HOW LOVE CAN BE
1964	Columbia DB 7423	NOW/HOW CAN YOU BELIEVE
1965	Columbia DB 7535	NO REGRETS/SEESAW OF DREAMS
1966	Columbia DB 7759	IT'S YOURSELF/SECRETS
1966	Columbia DB 7811	THE LIQUIDATOR/SUNSHINE
1966	United Artists UP 1134	DON'T TAKE THE LOVERS FROM THE WORLD/TAKE AWAY
1966	United Artists UP 1148	SHIRLEY/WHO COULD LOVE ME?
1967	United Artists UP 1173	THE IMPOSSIBLE DREAM/DO I LOOK LIKE A FOOL
1967	United Artists UP 1176	IF YOU GO AWAY/GIVE HIM MY LOVE
1967	United Artists UP 1192	BIG SPENDER/DANGEROUS GAMES
1968	United Artists UP 1207	THIS IS MY LIFE/WITHOUT A WORD
1968	United Artists UP 2254	TO GIVE/MY LOVE HAS TWO FACES
1968	United Artists UP 35083	DOES ANYBODY MISS ME/FA FA FA
1969	United Artists UP 35015	DOESN'T ANYBODY MISS ME/NOW YOU WANT TO BE LOVED
1969	Philips BF 1782	AS I LOVE YOU/KISS ME, HONEY HONEY, KISS ME
1970	United Artists UP 35094	SEA & SAND/WHAT ABOUT TODAY
1970	United Artists UP 35125	SOMETHING/EASY TO BE HARD
1971	United Artists UP 35156	FOOL ON THE HILL/WHAT ARE YOU DOING THE REST
1971	United Artists UP 35194	WHERE DO I BEGIN (LOVE STORY)/FOR THE LOVE OF HIM
1971	United Artists UP 35267	FOR ALL WE KNOW/WHAT'S DONE IS DONE
1972	United Artists UP 35293	DIAMONDS ARE FOREVER/PIECES OF DREAMS
1972	United Artists UP 35370	I'VE NEVER BEEN A WOMAN BEFORE /THE GREATEST PERFOR-MANCE OF MY LIFE
1972	United Artists UP 35459	AND I LOVE YOU SO/I DON'T KNOW HOW TO LOVE HIM
1972	United Artists UP 35424	BALLAD OF THE SAD YOUNG MAN/IF I SHOULD FIND LOVE AGAIN
1973	United Artists UP 35490	NEVER NEVER NEVER/DAY BY DAY
1973	United ArUsts UP 35557	MAKE THE WORLD A LITTLE YOUNGER/THE OLD FASHIONED WAY
1974	United Artists UP 35649	WHEN YOU SMILE/THE TROUBLE WITH HELLO IS GOODBYE
1975	United Artists UP 35837	GOOD, BAD BUT BEAUTIFUL/I'M NOTHING WITHOUT YOU
1975	United Artists UP 36007	LIVING/EVERYTHING THAT TOUCHES YOU
1976	United Artists UP 36102	NATALI/RUNAWAY
1976	United Artists UP 36200	CAN'T TAKE MY EYES OFF YOU/BORN TO LOSE
1977	United Artists UP 36247	I LET YOU LET ME DOWN AGAIN/RAZZLE DAZZLE
1977	United Artists UP 36260	YOU TAKE MY HEART AWAY/I LET YOU LET ME DOWN AGAIN
1979	United Artists UP 36502	THIS IS MY LIFE/THE MAGIC IS YOU
1979	United Artists UP 602	MOONRAKER (Main Title)/MOONRAKER
1980	HMV POP 2009	I (WHO HAVE NOTHING)/GOLDFINGER
1982	Applause APK 201	ALL BY MYSELF/WE DON'T CRY OUT LOUD
1984	Towerbell TOW 51	SOMETIMES/HE NEEDS ME
1984	Towerbell TOW 60	NATALIE/AS I LOVE YOU
1984	Towerbell TOW 62	I AM WHAT I AM/THIS IS MY LIFE
1985	Meteor MTEP 1001	MEMORY/I THOUGHT I'D RING YOU/THAT'S RIGHT/REMEMBER
1986	Towerbell TOW 87	TO ALL THE MEN I'VE EVER LOVED
1986	Towerbell TOW 90	THERE'S NO PLACE LIKE LONDON/BORN TO SING
1987	Mercury MER 253	THE RHYTHM DIVINE (with Yello)/Dr. Van Stelner (by Yello)
1996	East West EW072CD	'DISCO' LA PASSIONE (with Chris Rea)
1997	Wall Of Sound WALLD036	HISTORY REPEATING (with Propellerheads, various mixes)

1956

EXTENDED PLAYS

Year	Cat. No.	Title
1957	Philips BBE 12113	AT THE CAFE DE PARIS LONDON
1958	Philips BBE 12212	AS I LOVE YOU
1959	Philips BBE 12232	BLUES BY SHIRLEY BASSEY
1959	Philips BBE 12321	LOVE FOR SALE
1959	Columbia SEG 8027	THE FABULOUS SHIRLEY BASSEY
1959	HMV 7EG 8630	SHOWBOAT—EXCERPTS
1959	HMV 7EG 8642	SHOWBOAT—EXCERPTS NO.2
1960	Phillps BBE 12408	BLUES BY SHIRLEY BASSEY NO. 2
1960	Columbia SEG 8063	AS LONG AS HE NEEDS ME
1960	Columbia SEG 8068	THE FABULOUS SHIRLEY BASSEY NO. 2
1961	Columbia SEG 8116	SHIRLEY NO. 2
1961	Columbia SEG 8149	SHIRLEY NO. 3
1963	Columbia SEG 8252	THE HITS OF SHIRLEY BASSEY
1963	Columbia SEG 8258	IN OTHER WORDS
1963	Columbia SEG 8273	LET'S FACE THE MUSIC
1964	Columbia SEG 8296	I (WHO HAVE NOTHING)
1964	Columbia SEG 8315	SHIRLEY'S MOST REQUESTED SONGS
1964	Columbia SEG 8369	THE DYNAMIC SHIRLEY BASSEY
1960s	Columbia SEG 8098	SHIRLEY NO.1
1960s	Columbia SEG 8232	SHIRLEY BASSEY NO. 2
1960s	Columbla SEG 8165	SHIRLEY BASSEY
1960s	Columbia SEG 8404	LET'S FACE THE MUSIC NO.2
1960s	Columbia SEG 8200	TILL AND OTHER GREAT SONGS
1960s	Columbia SEG 8446	SHIRLEY STOPS THE SHOWS
1960s	Columbia SEG 8404	LET'S FACE THE MUSIC NO.2

ALBUMS

Year	Cat. No.	Title
1957	Phillps BBR 8130	BORN TO SING THE BLUES
1959	Columbia SCX 3287	THE FABULOUS SHIRLEY BASSEY
1961	Columbia 33SX 1286	SHIRLEY
1962	Columbia 33SX 1382	SHIRLEY BASSEY
1962	Columbia 33SX 1454	LET'S FACE THE MUSIC
1965	Columbia 33SX 1691	SHIRLEY STOPS THE SHOWS
1965	Columbia 33SX 1787	SHIRLEY BASSEY AT THE PIGALLE
1966	Wing WL 1079	THE BEST OF SHIRLEY BASSEY
1966	U A (S)ULP 1142	I'VE GOT A SONG FOR YOU
1967	UA (S)ULP 1160	AND WE WERE LOVERS
1968	Columbia SX/SCX 6204	TWELVE OF THOSE SONGS
1968	UA (S)ULP 1210	THIS IS MY LIFE
1968	Columbia SCX 6294	THE GOLDEN HITS OF SHIRLEY BASSEY
1969	UA UAS 29039	DOES ANYBODY MISS ME
1970	UA UAS 29095	LIVE AT THE TALK OF THE TOWN
1970	UA 4AS 29100	SOMETHING
1971	UA UAG 29149	SOMETHING ELSE
1972	UA UAD 60013/14	THE SHIRLEY BASSEY COLLECTION

Year	Cat. No.	Title
1972	UA UAS 29246	I CAPRICORN
1972	U A UAS 29385	AND I LOVE YOU SO
1972	Columbia SCX 6515	BROADWAY BASSEY'S WAY
1973	UA UAS 2947	NEVER NEVER NEVER
1974	UA USD 301/2	LIVE AT CARNEGIE HALL
1974	Columbia SCX 6569	THE VERY BEST OF SHIRLEY BASSEY
1975	UA UAS 29728	THE SHIRLEY BASSEY SINGLES ALBUM
1975	UA UAS 29881	GOOD BAD BUT BEAUTIFUL
1976	UA UAS 29944	LOVE, LIFE AND FEELINGS
1976	UA UAS 30011	THOUGHTS OF LOVE
1977	UA UAS 30037	YOU TAKE MY HEART AWAY
1978	UA SBTv- 60147/4E	25th ANNIVERSARY ALBUM
1978	UA UAS 30141	YESTERDAYS
1979	UA UATV 30230	THE MAGIC IS YOU
1979	UA UAG 30280	WHAT I DID FOR LOVE
1979	EMI EMTC 105	21 HIT SINGLES
1984	Towerbell TOWLP 7	I AM WHAT I AM
1985	President PRCV 117	PLAYING SOLITAIRE
1987	Con/isseur VSOPLP 110	BORN TO SING THE BLUES
1988	EMI EMS 1290	LET ME SING AND I'M HAPPY
1988	EMI DL 1140	THIS IS SHIRLEY BASSEY
1989	Mercury 838 033-1	LA MUJER

CDs

Year	Cat. No.	Title
1984	Vogue VG 600021	ALL BY MYSELF
1985	President PRCD1 117	PLAYING SOLITAIRE
1988	Towerbell CD TOW 7	I AM WHAT I AM
1988	EMI CDP 790 469-2	DIAMONDS (THE BEST OF SHIRLEY BASSEY)
1988	EMI CDP 790 422-2	LET ME SING AND I'M HAPPY
1988	EMI CDDL 1140	THIS IS SHIRLEY BASSEY
1991	Freestyle DIN CD21	KEEP THE MUSIC PLAYING
1989	Mercury 838 033-2	LA MUJER
1992	EMI CDDL 1221	LIVE: SHIRLEY BASSEY
1992	Telstar STACD 027/8	SOLID GOLD
1993	Icon ICOCD 007	THE BOND COLLECTION
1993	EMI CDDL 1239	COLLECTION: SHIRLEY BASSEY
1993	Target/BMG PRS23011	DIAMONDS ARE FOREVER
1993	Target/BMG PRS23010	GOLDFINGER
1993	Target/BMG DBP102002	SHIRLEY BASSEY: 40 GREAT SONGS
1993	EMI CDDPR 114	SHIRLEY BASSEY SINGS ANDREW LLOYD WEBBER
1994	PolyGram 514 347-2	CLASSIC TRACKS
1994	PolyGram 550 185-2	BORN TO SING
1994	EMI BASSEY 1	BASSEY—THE EMI/U.A. YEARS 1959-1979
1995	PolyGram 529 399-2	SINGS THE MOVIES
1996	EMI CDMFP 6252	20 OF THE BEST
1996	Polygram 533 712-2	THE SHOW MUST GO ON
1997	Artful CD10	THE BIRTHDAY CONCERT

1997